Augustus Jacobson

An Ounce of Prevention

to save America from having a government of the few

Augustus Jacobson

An Ounce of Prevention
to save America from having a government of the few

ISBN/EAN: 9783337314163

Printed in Europe, USA, Canada, Australia, Japan

Cover: Foto ©Suzi / pixelio.de

More available books at **www.hansebooks.com**

An Ounce of Prevention

By AUGUSTUS JACOBSON

Library of Progress, No. 3. Quarterly, $2.00 a year. June, 1892.

CHARLES H. KERR & CO., Pubs., 175 Dearborn St., Chicago

AN OUNCE OF PREVENTION

An Ounce of Prevention

To Save America from Having a Government
of the Few, by the Few and for the Few

BY

AUGUSTUS JACOBSON

CHICAGO
CHARLES H. KERR AND COMPANY
1892

The truth is that we are arrived at one of those periods in the progress of society when the constitution naturally undergoes a change, just as it did two centuries ago. It was impossible then for the king to keep down the higher part of the middle classes; it is impossible now to keep down the middle and lower parts of them. All that resistance to these natural changes can effect is to derange their operation, and make them act violently and mischievously, instead of healthfully, or at least harmlessly. The old state of things is gone past recall, and all the efforts of all the Tories cannot save it; but they may by their folly, as they did in France, get us a wild democracy or a military despotism in the room of it, instead of letting it change quietly into what is merely a new modification of the old state. One would think that people who talk against change were literally as well as metaphorically blind, and really did not see that everything in themselves and around them is changing every hour by the necessary laws of its being.

There is nothing so revolutionary, because there is nothing so unnatural and so convulsive to society, as the strain to keep things fixed, when all the world is, by the very law of its creation, in eternal progress; and the cause of all the evils of the world may be traced to that natural but most deadly error of human indolence and corruption — that our business is to preserve and not to improve. — DR. THOMAS ARNOLD, *Headmaster of Rugby, pending the Reform agitation in England, April,* 1831.

Quixotism or Utopianism, — that is another of the Devil's pet words. I believe the quiet admission which we are all of us ready to make, that because things have long been wrong it is impossible they should ever be right, is one of the most fatal sources of misery and crime from which this world suffers. Whenever you hear a man dissuading you from attempting to do well on the ground that perfection is "Utopian," beware of that man. Cast the word out of your dictionary altogether; there is no need for it. Things are either possible or impossible — you can easily determine which — in any given state of human science. If the thing is impossible, you need not trouble yourselves about it; if possible, try for it. — JOHN RUSKIN.

CONTENTS.

The Succession Tax 9

The Manual Training School 103

Appendix 165

AN OUNCE OF PREVENTION.

THE SUCCESSION TAX.

I.

The problem of problems in all ages has been the one which is beginning to press upon us now, and that is, How to prevent the few from getting all there is on the earth; how to keep the rich from getting richer and the poor from getting poorer; how to secure a fair distribution of property and the comforts and conveniences of life for all men and women.

Everybody wants to settle the labor question, but nobody is willing to sacrifice anything to settle it; nobody appears to be willing to pay out any money to settle it. The labor question will not be settled without sacrifice; it will not be settled without a large expenditure of money. To settle the labor question without sacrifice would be to get something for nothing. The settlement of the labor question will in some way have to be paid for.

II.

In the way of disturbance of business, the labor question has already cost this country hundreds of millions of dollars; and the agitation has hardly yet begun. There are now a million of men in the ranks of the Knights of Labor, with perhaps as many more enrolled in other labor organizations, with perpetual strikes and attendant lawlessness. Strikes and lawlessness cost money, not only to the strikers and the lawless, but to the general community. There is rarely a month now when the militia is not in active service; and it costs money to keep the militia in active service. In the month of May, 1886, there were two hundred militia companies in the course of formation in the State of Illinois; twenty regiments of a thousand men each, — twenty thousand men; as large an army as the Lieutenant-General of the United States commands. Pinkerton's private army[1] now numbers thousands of soldiers; and the large coal corporations maintain a private army of their own. The Pinkerton army and the

[1] See Appendix, I.

corporation army could probably upon any given day muster a greater number of effective men in New York, Pittsburgh, or Chicago, than the army of the United States. The agitation for the increase of the regular army is perpetual. In the midst of profound peace, the merchants of Chicago have raised several hundred thousand dollars to donate to the United States a tract of land in order to secure the location in Chicago of a military post; and the merchants have contributed this money solely from fear of lawlessness.

III.

Like the slavery question, which led to war, the labor question is an irrepressible conflict. The war between the States grew out of a labor question. It was a war for free labor. It was not till the day of Appomattox that in this country every laborer became a free man. There has rarely in the world been a question worth discussing that has not been in some way a labor question, and the world will probably never be without labor questions. The story of Adam and Eve in Paradise ends with a statement of the condition of the laborer of that early day: "In the sweat of thy face shalt thou eat bread till thou return unto the ground." Let us be fair. If we who do not labor with our hands and yet enjoy more of the good things of life than if we did, if we, all of us, nevertheless want shorter hours, more pay, and a vacation every year, why should we think it unreasonable for the man who gets $1.50 a day and never has a vacation to want shorter hours and more pay?

If there is any one thing that is praiseworthy in a man it is by all lawful means to seek to improve his condition, to provide for his children so as to give them a good start in life, and to provide for his own declining years.

IV.

I say that the settlement of the labor question will have to be paid for. In the case of slavery it would have been better for us, far better for us, to have paid for the slaves thrice over. Had we paid for the slaves thrice over we should then have saved thousands of millions of money, and we should have saved hundreds of thousands of lives and all the miseries of the war. The experience we had with the slavery question admonishes us to see to it that the labor question be settled peaceably and from the foundation. There were periodical settlements of the slavery question; there were compromises and settlements, in 1789, in 1820, and in 1850; but from first to last there was only one thing that could settle the slavery question, and that one thing was freedom for the slaves.

The freedom of all the slaves we could have bought outright with money. The solution of the labor question we can buy outright with money. And if we do not choose to spend the money directly now, we shall be forced to spend it indirectly later on. If we do not choose to spend the one dollar now, we shall be forced to spend the ten dollars later. The most expensive method of settling things is to settle them by means of lawlessness and soldiers.

V.

The demand of the man who is at the bottom for better things in life, is in the nature of things. It follows the Declaration of Independence and the enfranchisement of man as summer follows spring. It is a demand which sooner or later must be met, and it is in the interest of everybody that it should be met. Last year saw the enfranchisement of two millions of voters in England. This year has seen the agitation for Home Rule in Ireland, and the labor question is at the fore all over Europe and the United States. The idea that the general condition of man must be improved is in the air. It comes of the invention of gunpowder. It comes of the steam-engine. It comes of the printing-press. The movement is as irresistible as Niagara. We could n't stop it if we would, and I for one would n't stop it if I could. All that we can do about it is to see that all changes shall come without violence and without bloodshed, peaceably and beneficently. In this matter, as in all matters of social agitation, an ounce of prevention is worth a great deal more than a pound of cure.

VI.

In modern days there has been a steady amelioration in the condition of men who labor with their hands. The laboring-man has become politically free. He has obtained a small degree of intelligence. Shall he now permit the betterment of his condition to come to a stand-still? Why should he now permit his own improvement to come to a stand-still? But great as has been the amelioration of the common average man, the many are still the foot-ball of the few.

Society has been from the beginning of time and is now so organized as to get as much as possible out of the man who labors with his hands and to give him in return as little as possible. And when I speak of the man who labors with his hands, I mean not only the man who in city or country works for wages but likewise the farmer who works for himself. The man who works with his hands sells by the quantity and at the lowest possible price all he produces. Whatever he has to buy he buys at the highest retail price. In the game of life the cards are stocked against the man who labors with his hands.

VII.

The average life of the factory girl is only thirty years. The children who work in the factory look like little old men and women; and they are more vicious than old men and old women, — rotten before they are ripe. The child who enters a factory as an operative leaves hope behind. There are exceptions, — of course there are exceptions; yet the exceptions only prove the rule. The factory is a Moloch without mercy. The street-railroad sends the car horse, driver, and conductor alike to an early grave. The worker in lead soon becomes a chronic invalid, and the stone-cutter at thirty dies of consumption. In our cities there are hundreds of thousands of virtuous women who have abandoned all hope, for whom there is in the future nothing but ill-health, an early grave, or a hopeless old age of infirmity and want. Think of the women who eke out a miserable existence by sewing the clothes we wear. They sew from early morn till late at night, in summer burning with heat, in winter shivering with cold, with wretched and insufficient food, insufficient sleep, insufficient clothing, insufficient exercise, wretched surroundings, and never a whiff of fresh air. In by far the greater number of pursuits, the men and women who work with their hands risk their health and their lives with their every breath. And no matter how soon they sicken and die, others stand willing and anxious to take their places. The very chance to work is a boon. Among laboring people vice and crime are bred of want, and children are born destined inevitably for the brothel and the penitentiary. And the increase of wealth goes not to the man who works with his hands, but to the man who works with his head. The increase of wealth goes not to the worker, but to the schemer.

VIII.

Look at the invention of the steam-engine. Nearly all the wealth of modern times is earned by steam, which does for man his work. The wealth which steam earns should surely belong to all mankind. Do the many get the benefit of it? Not to any great extent. The money which steam earns goes into the hands not of the many, but of the few. If the money which steam earns went into the pockets of the many, to whom it belongs, we should to-day have an ideal people, a nation without an ignorant man and without a pauper.

The average working-man to-day by means of steam does as much work as ten men did a century ago, but he gets little better food, he gets little better clothing, he gets little better instruction, he lives in a hovel, he is out of employment periodically, and he and his are full of anxiety for the future. The money which steam earns, and which should go to the millions, goes to the few, and the many hopelessly drudge and slave on.

IX.

The wealth which steam has brought us has come upon us so suddenly that the people have not been prepared to take advantage of it. The common average man has been unable to get his share. While the wealth of the nation has increased in a ratio never before equalled, we have allowed the training of the people to stand substantially still. There not being general intelligence enough among the people to deal with the problem, from want of knowledge, from want of foresight, we have allowed the enormous wealth brought us by steam to be put upon a card and seized by the few. It is as if a few Hebrew Jay Goulds had seized upon all the manna in the Wilderness. Moses wisely did not permit the manna to be thus cornered. Moses made wise regulations which prevented the cornering of the manna in the Wilderness. But our wealth, which is our manna, has been cornered. In this land, in which there is an abundance for everybody, multitudes are suffering for the necessaries of life. It is high time to see to it that there shall be a fairer distribution of the good things of this world.

X.

To achieve better things for the man who is the under-dog in life's fight, the one thing that can never be of any use is lawlessness. A cause which, in this land of free speech, proceeds in any other way than the good old Anglo-Saxon and Anglo-American way of convincing by argument, is lost from the start. If a cause is good the majority will eventually be convinced. The end and aim and object of government in this country is to secure the greatest good of the greatest number. In this country it is impossible to keep common-sense from being eventually enacted into law. The people may be slow to see where their interests lie, but when they do see it the measure which furthers their interest becomes immediately the law of the land. If the man who is the lawmaker for the time being refuses to enact into law the will of the people, there is always another man who is very anxious to become a law-maker upon the express condition of doing what the people want.

In the right to vote and to levy taxes, the struggling multitude have the power not only peaceably to right every wrong under which they suffer, but they have moreover the power to provide peaceably for their own indefinite elevation.

The labor question is one of hours and wages, but it is not a mere question of fewer hours and more pay. Suppose that every laboring man in the country could have immediately more pay for less work; suppose that all that laboring men now ask for were granted; that would not permanently settle the labor question. It is not a question involving merely hours and wages.

XI.

As in the case of the slavery question, no compromise could settle it, nothing but freedom could settle it; so it is with the labor question,—nothing but a higher state of existence for the subject of the controversy can settle the labor question. There will be strikes and there will be boycotts, and there will be arbitration, and there will be a thousand schemes; but there is only one thing that can permanently settle the labor question, and that is the individual improvement and elevation of the man who has to labor with his hands.

There is a very simple way which would help us out of our present troubles and smooth the road for those who are to come after us. It is a simple way, but for all that it would be a revolution. To a man who has been ill for years, good health is a revolution. Of that sort would be this revolution. It would be a revolution much greater than any hitherto known; but it would be a peaceful Anglo-Saxon revolution. While the revolution was going on, everybody would go about his business. There would be no lawlessness, no destruction of property, nobody would be maimed, nobody would be wounded, nobody would be killed.

XII.

There was graduated, June, 1886, at the Manual Training School at the corner of Twelfth Street and Michigan Avenue, Chicago, a class of boys who are an entirely new product in the world. They were boys about eighteen years of age, who three years before had never touched tools with a view to becoming skilled in their use. These boys had drawn the plans for several steam-engines. They had drawn the patterns on paper. They had made the patterns in wood. They had been forced to have the castings done by other hands, because there were then in the school no facilities for making castings. They would have made the castings if there had been facilities for doing so. The boys had done the chipping and the filing and the lathe-work. They had put together their engines. At the word of command steam was turned on, and the engines began to run. One of the engines made by the boys is now running every day in the school.

These boys had not neglected their books. They were ready to stand up and be examined side by side with boys who in the ordinary high school had devoted all their time to books.

XIII.

The manual training school is not a contrivance for making more mechanics. It is a contrivance for developing individual power. The education of the manual training school is just as serviceable for the scholars who are not to be mechanics as it is for those who are to be mechanics. It is just as serviceable for the boy who is to be a lawyer, physician, dentist, or what not, as for the boy who is to make shoes. The education of the training school is in the direction of the polytechnic school of the present time. Having the mental training of a graduate of a high school, the graduate of a manual training school will not compete with the average wage-worker, because he will be able to do very much better for himself. As things are now, the average graduate of a manual training school will earn at twenty-one years of age $750 a year; and that keeps him away above competing with the average wage-worker. The wage-workers used to think that they must save themselves from competition by prohibiting apprentices from learning trades. By letting the apprentices learn so much more than the wage-workers know, the same object is effected. The man who earns $1.50 a day strikes periodically because he is constantly underbid in the market. The market is crowded with $1.50 men. The man who has from three to five dollars a day rarely strikes, because he has things more his own way. There are fewer of his kind. Instead of his being obliged to hunt for a place the place hunts for him. The manual training school raises a boy above the competition of the masses of men.

XIV.

Manual training is now being introduced in the public schools of Chicago, and manual training schools are springing up all over the land. The people no sooner see manual training than they want it for their children. If all the children of the United States could have the manual training school education, they would be raised to a grade where there is no labor question. There is always plenty of room higher up.

The first step towards a remedy for the poor condition of the world's hand-workers lies in raising the grade of their intelligence, the grade of their skill, the grade of their work, and as a consequence the grade of their ability and power to earn money. The first step towards a remedy for the poor condition of the world's hand-workers lies in training their brains together with their hands, and letting the product of their labor be the product both of skilled hands and of trained brains. The first step lies in increasing the earning capacity of the individual.

At the present time, for the children of laboring people after they are ten or twelve years old, school facilities such as now exist are only a hollow mockery. There is no earthly use in additional school facilities unless the children are supplied with the means of availing themselves of those facilities. The necessity is upon the children to earn their livelihood; and of what use are school facilities to children who must work for their daily bread from early morn till dewy eve?

XV.

My proposition is that the manual training school shall be made a part of the American public school system, as it already is in Chicago, Toledo, Philadelphia, and other places, and that to enable all children to get the benefit of the school, parents or guardians shall be paid for keeping the children at school throughout the public course, including the high school or manual training school. The compensation should begin at the child's twelfth and continue till his twentieth year.

1st year	$50
2d "	75
3d "	100
4th "	125
5th "	150
6th "	175
7th "	225
8th "	300

The proposition includes boys and girls. In Toledo and Philadelphia, where manual training has been introduced into the public schools, experiments are being made which will eventually make the manual training as serviceable for girls as it already is for boys. In Philadelphia and Toledo girls are being taught cooking, sewing, and many of the household arts.[1]

[1] See Appendix, II.

XVI.

The expense would be enormous, of course. The remedy is an extraordinary one, and extraordinary means would have to be resorted to to carry it into effect. The expense could not be met by any taxation in vogue at present, but it could be met by a graduated succession tax upon estates. To collect such a tax would cost nothing of any consequence, because no new officers would be needed to levy or collect it. In war times we had a succession tax, and it never failed to be collected; simply because the probate judge could declare no estate settled until the tax had been paid. The tax, until paid, was a lien upon all the property of the estate. The tax could not be avoided. It never failed to be paid. It was upon personal property only,— ¾%, 1½, 3, 4, and 5%, depending upon the relationship of the party inheriting to the deceased. The law was passed by Congress in 1861, amended in 1862, and both acts were signed by Abraham Lincoln as President.

They will be found in the United States Statutes at Large, Vol. XII., page 485.

"Sect. 111. And be it further enacted, That any person or persons having in charge or trust, as administrators, executors, or trustees of any legacies or distributive shares arising from personal property of any kind whatsoever, where the whole amount of such personal property as aforesaid shall exceed the sum of $1,000 in actual value, passing from any person who may die after the passage of this act, possessed of such property either by will or by the intestate laws of any State or Territory, or any part of such property or interest therein, transferred by deed, grant, bargain, sale, or gift made or intended to take effect in possession or enjoyment after the death of the grantor or bargainor, to any person or persons or to any body or bodies politic or corporate, in trust or otherwise, shall be and hereby are, made subject to a duty or tax, to be paid to United States, as follows, that is to say : —

1. Where the person or persons entitled to any beneficial interest in such property shall be the lineal issue or lineal ancestor, brother or sister, to the person who died possessed of such property, as aforesaid, at and after the rate of seventy five cents for each and every hundred dollars of the clear value of such interest in such property.

2. Where the person or persons entitled to any beneficial interest in such property shall be a descendant of a brother or sister of the person who died possessed as aforesaid, at and after the rate of one dollar and fifty cents for each and every hundred dollars of the clear value of such interest.

3. Where the person or persons entitled to any beneficial interest in such property shall be a brother or sister of the father or mother, or a descendant of the brother or sister of the father or mother of the person who died possessed as aforesaid, at and after the rate of three dollars for each and every hundred dollars of the clear value of such interest.

4. Where the person or persons entitled to any beneficial interest in such property shall be a brother or sister of the grandfather or grandmother, or a descendant of the brother or sister of the grandfather or grandmother of the person who died possessed as aforesaid, at and after the rate of four dollars for each and every hundred dollars of the clear value of such interest.

5. Where the person or persons entitled to any beneficial interest in such property shall be in any other degree of collateral consanguinity than is hereinbefore stated, or shall be a stranger in blood to the person who died possessed, as aforesaid, or shall be a body politic or corporate, at and after the rate of five dollars for each and

every hundred dollars of the clear value of such interest. Provided: That all legacies or property passing by will or by the laws of any State or Territory to husband or wife of the person who died possessed, as aforesaid, shall be exempt from tax or duty."

XVII.

In war times we had a graduated income tax, so that a graduated tax is not new to the American people. The succession tax and the graduated tax are not going to upset the country. They are both things that have already been. The principle that a large accumulation should pay at a higher rate than a small accumulation was established in war times. The income tax was —

    5% on all incomes over $600 and under $5,000
    7½%   "   "   "   5,000 "   "   10,000
    10%   "   "   "   10,000

The law was passed in 1864, and signed by Abraham Lincoln as President. It may be found in the United States Statutes at Large, Vol. XIII., page 281.

"SECT. 116. And be it further enacted, That there shall be levied, collected and paid annually upon the annual gains, profits or income of every person residing in the United States, or of any citizen of the United States residing abroad, whether derived from any kind of property, rents, interests, dividends, salaries, or from any profession, trade, employment, or vocation, carried on in the United States or elsewhere, or from any other source whatever, except as hereinafter mentioned, if such annual gains, profits, or income, exceed the sum of six hundred dollars, a duty of five per centum on the excess over six hundred dollars and not exceeding five thousand dollars ; and a duty of seven and one half of one per centum per annum on the excess over five thousand dollars and not exceeding ten thousand dollars ; and a duty of ten per centum on the excess over ten thousand dollars."

The income tax was, to be sure, levied in war times and under the exigencies of war times. The tax which I propose is to prevent war times. " Let us have peace." The income tax was odious because the scrupulous paid, and the unscrupulous escaped by swearing falsely. A succession tax is a fair method of taxation because nobody can escape paying it. All must pay, and all must pay alike in proportion to the size of the estate.

The State of New York has a graduated succession tax passed by the Legislature of New York, June 10, 1885. It may be found in the Laws of New York, 1885, 108th Session, Chapter 483, page 820, and is entitled " An Act to tax gifts, legacies, and collateral inheritances in certain cases."

"SECT. 1. After the passage of this act, all property which shall pass by will or by the intestate laws of this State from any person who may die seized or possessed of the same while being a resident of the State, or which property shall be within this State, or any part of such property, or any interest therein, or income therefrom, transferred by deed, grant, sale or gift, made or intended to take effect in possession or enjoyment after the death of the grantor or bargainor, to any person or persons, or to a body politic or corporate, in trust or otherwise, or by reason whereof any person, or body politic or corporate shall become beneficially entitled, in possession or expectancy, to any property, or to the income thereof, other than to or for the use of father, mother, husband, wife, children, brother and sister and lineal descendants born in lawful wedlock, and the wife or widow of a son and the husband of a daughter, and the societies, corporations and institutions now exempted by law from taxation, shall be and is subject to a tax of five dollars on every hundred dollars of the clear market value of such property, and at and after the same rate for any less amount, to be paid to the treasurer of the proper county, and in the city and county of New York to the Comptroller thereof, for the use of the State, and all administrators, executors and trustees shall be liable for any and all such taxes, until the same shall have been paid, as hereinafter directed. Provided: That an estate which may be valued at a less sum than five hundred dollars shall not be subject to said duty or tax."[1]

This law establishes a succession tax, so far as it goes, and it establishes a graduated succession tax because a very small estate is exempt while a larger one is taxed.

[1] See Appendix, III.

XVIII.

The tax which I propose would be graduated, — small on small amounts, and larger as the amounts increase.

Rate				Lower			Upper
¼% on all estates less than				$25,000			
½% on all estates above				$25,000	and less than		$50,000
¾%	"	"	"	50,000	"	"	100,000
1%	"	"	"	100,000	"	"	200,000
2%	"	"	"	200,000	"	"	300,000
3%	"	"	"	300,000	"	"	400,000
4%	"	"	"	400,000	"	"	500,000
5%	"	"	"	500,000	"	"	600,000
6%	"	"	"	600,000	"	"	700,000
7%	"	"	"	700,000	"	"	800,000
8%	"	"	"	800,000	"	"	900,000
9%	"	"	"	900,000	"	"	1,000,000

Ten per cent above a million; one per cent additional for each additional hundred thousand, up to fifty per cent on five millions or any sum above five millions.

This tax would not and could not fall heavily upon anybody, because where there was no estate there would be no tax. It would not annoy the man of business struggling with difficulties, because it would not be levied upon business, but only upon accumulations actually left at death. If the estate were small it would be a very small tax, at a very small rate. If the estate were large the estate would pay a large tax, at a rate high in proportion to its size. If there were no accumulations there would be no tax.

XIX.

I will not here go into wearisome details. It is enough to say that the proceeds of the tax would cover the proposed expenditure. The tax would be sufficient for the proposed education, but no more than sufficient. The tax would probably, at the rates named, be equal to the expense of the education; and the expense of the education would probably be equal to the proceeds of the tax. The tax would at present yield from three to six millions annually in Chicago, and from twenty-five to fifty millions annually in New York City.

But can this state of things be brought about? Have the people the right to make such laws? The people can make whatever laws they like; and when made, laws must be obeyed by all. The only question is, Would such a law be expedient? Would such a law be for the general good of all the people?

XX.

In addition to the succession tax which I propose it would be greatly for the interest of the people of the United States to establish some of the rules of inheritance of the Code Napoleon, under which the immense subdivision of estates in France has taken place. It is the law in France that if a man has one child that child takes by law one half of the father's estate. The father can dispose otherwise, as he likes, of the other half, but he can dispose of no more than one half. The father can dispose only of what would be the share of one child. If he has two children he can dispose of one third of his estate, if three children of one fourth, if four children of one fifth, and so on. The children have their remedy at law to recover their portion of their father's estate. There are very few wills made in France, because the law disposes so wisely of estates and leaves people so little liberty in willing away their property. There is rarely in France a contest over a will; the law disposes of the property, and it goes to the children, and not, as so often in this country, to the lawyers. If this wise law had been in force in this country, the Vanderbilt and Astor estates could never have become what they are; and if this were now the law the Vanderbilt, Astor, and Gould fortunes must soon be scattered among many heirs, instead of being held together as a menace to the business interests and liberties of this people.[1]

[1] See Appendix, IV.

XXI.

The purpose being fully understood, I believe that the people would gladly vote the succession tax. The moderately well-to-do would gladly favor it in view of its application, because it would be so obviously for their advantage. Upon an estate of $1,000 the tax would be only $2.50. Upon an estate of less than $25,000 the tax could not exceed $62.50. Upon an estate of less than $50,000 the tax could not exceed $250. Upon an estate of less than $75,000 the tax could not exceed $562.50. Upon an estate of $100,000 the tax would be $1,000. Upon an estate of $199,000 the tax would be $1,900. Upon an estate of $299,000 the tax would be $5,980. Upon an estate of $399,000 the tax would be $11,970. Upon an estate of $499,000 the tax would be $19,960. Upon an estate of $1,000,000 the tax would be $100,000. Upon an estate of $2,000,000 the tax would be $400,000. Upon an estate of $3,000,000, $900,000. Upon $4,000,000, $1,600,000 ; and upon an estate of $5,000,000 and upwards, the tax would be one half of the estate. The larger the estate, the more easily could the tax be borne. In the nature of things the tax could never fall heavily upon anybody, because the tax would be in proportion to the size of the estate, and where there was no estate there would be no tax.

XXII.

Without wealth there can be no intelligence. The wealth of a country must produce the intelligence of that country, or there will be no intelligence. This country cannot peaceably get along with the intelligence we now have. The best proof of that is that we are not getting along peaceably. No matter in whose hands the wealth is, intelligence sufficient to enable us to live in peace must be paid for and produced. With the means at hand to prevent it, we cannot afford to let our institutions succumb to chaos and anarchy. That in this land of liberty children should be foredoomed to starvation, to vice, and to crime, as they are in lands of despotism, would make of liberty a delusion and a snare, and would make us all feel that the less we said about liberty the better. That is not what is in store for the children who are to be born in poverty on this generous American soil. The question is not what the few would like. The question is what is for the interest of the many. The welfare of the people is the supreme law. The welfare of the people is above everything else. All private considerations have to yield to the welfare of the people. Unless the wealth of the country shall in the manner proposed, or in some similar manner, be made to respond to the educational needs of the country, all the beggarliness, degradation, and hopelessness of European life will be upon us.

Except for purposes of power and display, it makes no difference whatever whether a family has five millions or ten millions of money. Five millions will give them everything they can use, just as well as ten millions. Money which enables people to dispense with care, forethought, and labor, is a curse rather than a blessing. It may be safely asserted that more young people are rendered worthless and ruined than are benefited by large inheritances.

XXIII.

What is called society in this country imitates to the extent of its ability English society, and high English society gives every evidence of being the most corrupt institution on the earth. Contrary to the general opinion, high society in France, because it is comparatively poor, is sweet and pure compared to society in England. English society is accessible to everybody who has a long purse. English society is a wonderful illustration of the mischief that Satan finds for idle hands to do. In England, the higher you get socially the lower you get morally; and that is the condition of things which great fortunes tend to introduce into this country.

Horace Greeley was more than half right in saying that a man worth more than a million is a nuisance. Money in superabundance only enables the possessor to lead a life of self-indulgence. That a class of habitual do-nothings should grow up here, to poison life for the workers, flies in the face of all American tradition and aspiration. It is good public policy for the law to step in and prevent it, as it is for the law to step in and prevent the establishment of any other public nuisance.

The law of inheritance of the Code Napoleon, which has now been the law of France nearly a hundred years, coupled with the succession tax which I propose, would immediately put an end to all excessively large fortunes in this country.

XXIV.

If the law in New York were now what I propose, the William H. Vanderbilt estate would furnish over a hundred millions of dollars for the education of the people. Had this been the law of New York in 1875, the estate of Commodore Vanderbilt would at that time have furnished for education from thirty to fifty millions. And if that amount of money had been taken from Commodore Vanderbilt's estate in 1875, the present Vanderbilt fortune would have been impossible. If, then, the rest of the fortune had been divided among all of Commodore Vanderbilt's children, share and share alike, instead of being given substantially all to William H. Vanderbilt alone, all the cornering of things that has been done all these years by means of the Vanderbilt fortune would have been impossible.

Not a man, woman, or child of the name of Vanderbilt would have been in the slightest degree any the less comfortable if the tax had been collected, and the Vanderbilt fortune equally divided among the Commodore's children. We are apt to think that only poverty is brutalizing. Excessive wealth appears to be equally so. Nothing short of so much money could have caused old Commodore Vanderbilt to cut off all his children but one, without their having given him the slightest cause for it. If the Commodore's money had been evenly distributed among his children after paying the tax I propose, there can be no doubt that the happiness of the Vanderbilt family would have been far greater than it has been.

Would this tax be unjust to the Vanderbilts? The Vanderbilt estate is one of the many vast accumulations earned by steam. Without steam the accumulation would not have been possible. The Vanderbilts did not invent steam. The Vanderbilt estate is one of the vast accumulations gotten together at the expense of the people by stock-watering. The Vanderbilt estate was never fairly earned, as a man earns money in legitimate business. As a matter of fact, among the fortunes running up into the many millions there is not one in twenty that is honestly earned in legitimate business. The Vanderbilt money is tainted. The immense pile is the result of some honest industry, and of a vast deal of legislative, judicial, and every other form of corruption and imposition on the people. But if this tax would be unjust to the Vanderbilts, would it be as brutally unjust as it was for Commodore Vanderbilt to deprive nearly all his children of any substantial share in his estate? There would be no injustice to the Vanderbilts in the succession tax. Had the law as I propose it existed at the time, it would have done that justice to Commodore Vanderbilt's children which he himself did not choose to do.

XXV.

Would this measure be just to all? Government is not a matter of absolute justice. Government at best is only a matter of expediency. This measure is expedient. It would produce no unhappiness, and it would produce an immense deal of happiness. That part of the earth which we inhabit would become less and less of a vale of tears with each year. With the very rich people there would not at any rate be any question of suffering. They would still be very comfortable and happy after paying a succession tax. They would be much happier paying fifty per cent than if the amount inherited were so small that the rate would be only one per cent. There is no question of justice involved at all. There is involved in the whole matter only a question of expediency. But let us admit for the sake of argument that there is a question of justice. Let us admit for the sake of argument that it would be unjust towards men who are now many times millionnaires, to enact, to take effect immediately, the law which would upon their death take for public uses from ten to fifty per cent of their estates. Then let us suppose the law to be enacted so that the rate of tax over and above ten per cent should take effect not till the year 1925, leaving all our very rich men forty years in which to die and thus have their property escape the tax. Until 1925, then, the man of fifty millions would pay only at the same rate as the man of one million. That would apparently be unjust too; but it is all a matter not of justice but of expediency. But surely, after 1925, the law having been established many years and great wealth having been acquired under it and subject to it, nobody could then complain with any degree of fairness.

To suit the notions of those who always desire the welfare of mankind to be postponed to a more convenient season, the whole law might be enacted to take effect after we shall all be dead and gone, and then, maybe, its enactment would be less difficult. The importation of negroes as slaves was abolished in this way, to take effect in 1808, by the Constitution of the United States adopted in 1787, leaving twenty-one years more time wherein to increase the evil which was to give us four years of war. I would rather have the law which I propose take effect forty years hence than not to have it at all, but if it were well done 't were well 't were done quickly.

I put this measure upon the ground of expediency, but I believe it to be pre-eminently just. I believe it to be a measure which would increase in this country the tendency of things to " make for righteousness." With a population so intelligent and efficient as it would produce, the reform of the civil service would become an easy matter. There would be less intemperance. Good tendencies of individuals are strengthened by thorough training of mind and body, and evil ones are diminished by the same means. Besides, intemperance is often the result of helplessness and hopelessness, — of seeing no way out. With individual power to achieve things come hope and strength, and with hope and strength and faith in the future come temperance and a firmer character all around. Women with their own way to make in the world would find themselves better fitted for the work of the world. With ability to do many things, they would more easily find the one thing to do, and therefore they would find the world's roads easier. All reforms and improvements, all good causes, would be helped by this measure. It is broader than any and all of them.

XXVI.

The very rich man would say that he should be permitted to do what he likes with his own. That he cannot do even now. The law interferes with him at every step and tells him what he may do with his own and what he must not do. The test of what a man may do with his own is that what he does must not be contrary to public policy; what he does must not be contrary to the welfare of the people. People used to entail their property so as to have it descend to the first-born male. That was once the case with landed property in this country, and it is still the case in England. We have done away with entails and primogeniture on the ground that they are contrary to public policy. Public policy decides what a man may do with his property; and to say nothing of the object for which this money is sorely needed, fortunes running up into the hundreds of millions of money are contrary to public policy if ever there was anything contrary to public policy.

The very rich people would object both to the succession tax and to rules of inheritance which would prevent what has been done in the Vanderbilt and Astor estates; but the very rich people, like the rest of us, live in a country of majority rule, and for the general good we all have to submit to things that we do not like; and the very rich people must not stand in the way of the general good.

XXVII.

Nearly all rich men, at least nearly all those whose estates do not run up into the many millions, do as much for benevolent objects as the proposed succession tax would take from their estates. It may be said to be a custom in the United States for people of large means to bequeath money for benevolent objects; and as wealth increases the custom is more and more observed. Nowhere else on earth do people of wealth give away money as freely as they do here. In the city of Chicago alone there are at this very moment bequests not yet carried into effect amounting to at least five millions of dollars. Washington De Pauw of Evansville, Indiana, died recently, bequeathing $1,250,000 to the De Pauw University of Greencastle, Indiana. This bequest is in addition to large sums previously given by him to the same institution, by reason whereof the University had changed its name from Asbury to De Pauw.[1] But in carrying out their benevolent ideas people of wealth rarely act with much wisdom, and rarely in such a

[1] See Appendix, V.

manner as to accomplish much good. They cause to be erected and established libraries where there are no readers, and colleges where there are no students. Well-meaning and benevolent rich men have endowed and established, at the South, innumerable so-called colleges where young colored people are wasting their time and strength in learning Latin and Greek! How could anything be more absurd? These things are not to be wondered at. Men who know how to accumulate large sums generally have their thoughts fully occupied with business, and have but little time to give to the progress of the world. When Professor Agassiz was offered $100,000 to lecture, he said that he had no time to make money, that he needed all his time for thought. Rich men have no time for high thought, they need all their time to make money. Men who have accumulated millions keep on accumulating while they can, because generally that is all they know how to do. Generally their tastes have not been developed in any direction other than that of money getting. First they begin to accumulate to provide for a rainy day, then for a competency, then for a fortune, then it becomes an excitement and amusement, and it ends by being the only thing they are capable of. I knew a very wealthy man many times a millionnaire, who, dying recently, inquired with almost his dying breath for the last market quotations of stocks. There are exceptions of course; there are exceptions to all rules. Rich men lead in killing hogs and bullocks, in selling dry goods and groceries, in cornering things, and in all material enterprises, but not in the world of thought. As to the world of thought very rich men, engrossed with business, are situated very much as convicts in the penitentiary are situated as to the news of the day. A stray bit of thought may reach the rich man, as a stray bit of news may reach the convict, but that is all. The natural-born accumulator subordinates everything to the one supremely important object of getting things of which he has no need. It is not to be wondered at that men of this stamp, even when seeking to do benevolent things with their money, fail entirely in accomplishing their object. I say, and I say it without fear of contradiction, that by many such men a law once enacted and fairly carried out, which would take from their estates a reasonable share and secure with it the greatest good of the greatest number, would be regarded as a boon. In the current number (December, 1886), of the "North American Review," Mr. Pierre Lorillard has an article in which he advocates a legacy tax of 10 per cent on all estates above $200,000, upon the express ground that such a tax would tend to put an end to excessive fortunes. Mr. Lorillard is, as we all know, not a sentimentalist, not a socialist, but a very wealthy manufacturer of chewing and smoking tobacco, whose estate would have to pay a very considerable amount of money under such a law as he advocates.

The late Mr. Samuel J. Tilden, one of the cunningest lawyers in the world, left the greater portion of his estate for benevolent purposes, and now less cunning lawyers than Mr. Tilden was are busy setting aside his will. If the law had taken for public education, in the manner which I propose, one half of Mr. Tilden's estate, there would still have been left enough to give to his relatives much more than he meant to give them, and then there would still have been left enough wherewith to perpetuate Mr. Tilden's memory.

Senator Stanford's case is another one in point. By founding a college with twenty millions of dollars he is seeking to have his name go down to posterity as a benefactor of his race. But of colleges of a high order there are already enough. It is a very stupid way to spend so much money, for only a very limited number of educated men and women can be produced by an institution of that sort. The way to make good education general is to give to all a good foundation for an education; and then those whose bias is towards learning will struggle forward and help themselves to the highest possible education. Senator Stanford's twenty millions at three per cent would yield yearly six hundred thousand dollars, and six hundred thousand dollars would, on the basis I propose, educate in manual training schools four thousand pupils yearly; and out of the four thousand pupils thus started upon the road towards learning, there would be eventually a greater number of highly-educated men and women than Senator Stanford's money will ever produce, — leaving the manual training school education of the rest of the pupils a net gain.

When a sufficient provision has been made out of an estate for public uses, to be spent not to suit individual caprice but in the manner most conducive to public welfare, then the relatives of the deceased should have the rest, and the memory of the dead man be left to stand upon its merits or demerits as the case may be. The Vanderbilt perpetuity, the Tilden act of self-glorification are contrary to the interests of the people, contrary to public policy, and the law should step in and put an end to them.

XXVIII.

The proposition is not to take by taxation private property, without compensation. Never before in the world has such compensation been given for property as there would be for the amount of this tax. The compensation would be in the increased happiness of mankind. The rich would not become poor, and the poor would not become rich, but everybody would be more comfortable. This tax would not make life harder for one single human being, but it would make life easier for millions. The compensation would be in a peaceable and orderly society which would never be at war with itself. The compensation would be in perfect security of property. The more property a man has, the greater is his anxiety about its security, and he can well afford to pay a higher rate for security in proportion to his anxiety. Now, as the number of men holding property becomes larger so does the security of property increase. Where the many are hopeless about acquiring property there can be no security of property. If to make property secure you once begin to increase the army there will be no end of it, and soldiers are far more expensive than schoolmasters. It is much cheaper to make good citizens by means of schoolmasters than it is to shoot bad citizens by means of soldiers. And we must have either more schoolmasters or more soldiers. The proposition which I have set forth would without any additional soldiers fill the large house with peaceful security; it would fill the small house with hope, self-respect, aspiration, pluck. It means security of property for those who have it; and for those who have it not it means a fair chance to acquire property. And therefore it means the highest possible security of property.

The security of property which the high education of all the people would produce would make the succession tax the best possible investment for all. With dynamite and other modern means of destruction at hand it is in the interest of everybody that the rising generation shall grow up to be intelligent and efficient men and women. If we go on at the present rate, it will be only a short time before we shall be as afraid of the rising of the laboring men as the South used to be of negro insurrections. But take the children of the anarchists condemned to be hanged and make them intelligent and efficient American citizens, and they will not wish to march under the red flag. They will wish to march only under the flag under which they were made intelligent and efficient men and women. Can any state of things be conceived which the great body of the common people would fight harder to maintain? This proposition is quite as much in the interest of the rich as it is in the interest of the poor.

XXIX.

This measure is by no means directed against the rich. I am speaking of the opposition of the rich because some of them will oppose the succession tax as being aimed and directed against them, whereas it is really in their interest and in the interest of everybody. The rich men of the present generation will all be in their coffins in a few years. They can neither much help nor hinder any measure. The barefooted and impecunious descendants of many of them will be glad enough to find the world's roads easier. The policy which I propose is not invented to despoil anybody, but to bless everybody. I am proposing a policy to affect mainly men who have not yet begun to accumulate and men who have not yet been born. I am speaking of a proposition broad enough for the universe, and altogether too broad to be directed against any individual or individuals. I am speaking of a policy for all men and for all time. This measure would bear comparatively little on the present generation. It is for the immense future. Once established, the generations born under it would never think of changing it, because its effects upon humanity would be beneficial beyond anything ever conceived.

XXX.

This measure, more than anything else that could be devised, would put an end to the arraying of the masses against the classes. The very best thing that wealthy people can get for their money is high education for their children, and this measure once established the poor would be able to get that, too. Instead of having the fierce hatred for the possessors of wealth which is now developing in this country, the poor would say of a rich man: Let him go on accumulating money; at his death some of his money will be our money for the education of our children ; and the more he accumulates the more we shall get.

This measure once established, the cities, instead of being sores upon the body politic, would be filled with a rising generation of intelligent youth that would reform politics. Corruption in our city government would measurably cease. Where do corrupt aldermen and legislators mainly come from? They come from, and are elected in, sections of the city noted for the ignorance of the inhabitants. The sections of the city where the most intelligent people live generally elect intelligent, honest, and fair-minded representatives. The ignorant sections elect ignorant, corrupt, and thievish representatives. Like master, like man.

In a few years we should have the most intelligent population on the earth. We should have a population altogether too intelligent for lawlessness.

If all the children of the United States, the children of the laboring population as well as the children of the well-to-do, could have this education, our boast that in this country there are equal opportunities for all would come very near being true.

This training of the young into intelligence and efficiency, accompanied with payment to their parents for the time spent in getting the training, would go very far towards solving the labor question. There is nothing else that would go so far towards solving it. Regardless of the labor question, this would be a good thing to do. If there were no labor question at all, it would still be the very best thing to do. But there is a labor question, and so long as we do not solve it by education it will be and abide and remain with us forever, an irrepressible conflict.

Instead of going for a mere pittance into the coal mine, the mill, or the factory, to be dwarfed physically, mentally, and morally, by long hours, over-work, and evil associations, the children of the poor, for like wages wherewith to buy bread, would gladly crowd into the schools. Getting them into the schools and keeping them there throughout the public course would bring trained to the front all the brains and ability born in the community. It would bring capacity to the front, from the Five Points as well as from Murray Hill. It would light up with bright hopes and aspirations for the children the poorest hovel. It would mean fewer tramps, fewer paupers, fewer hovels, and more comfortable people. More than ever before it would make of this land for struggling humanity an earthly paradise.

XXXI.

If this proposition were carried into effect it would immediately settle the child-labor question. The children would be at school, where they ought to be. The orphans and the fatherless would be educated. The children of drunkards would be educated. Charity would still cover a multitude of sins, but charity would be relieved from nearly all responsibility toward the rising generation. The young have not sinned by coming into the world, and charity should not be troubled about them. This measure enacted, charity would be left to its legitimate function of relieving distress. Charity would have nothing to do with education ; a good education would become the birthright of every American child.

The civilizing home influence of children trained up to the point of a complete high-school education would entirely change the present aspect of the homes of the country. In thousands of homes the well-trained children would lead their parents into gentler and better ways. Even people who had no appreciation of education would educate their children if paid for doing it. Nowadays people leave their children in ignorance, because they cannot afford the expense of educating them. But under my proposition it would be cheaper for parents to educate their children than to leave them in ignorance. The poorer the parents, the more anxious would they be to educate their children, and the more certain would they be to do it. Poor parents would make life easier for themselves simply by educating their children. Between the ages of twelve and twenty each child would draw each year an average of one hundred and fifty dollars for support while being educated. If there were four children in a family their aggregate school-years after twelve would be thirty-two; and the family would draw for their schooling from the public fund, during say sixteen years, four thousand eight hundred dollars. The intelligent and efficient young would take care of and provide for the old and infirm. Of the misery of the world whose origin is in want, one half would disappear. "Verily I say unto you, inasmuch as ye have done it unto one of the least of these my brethren, ye have done it unto me." Gathering the children from the highways and byways, from the very gutter, rescuing them from vice and crime, putting them in the way of being useful men and women, — would this measure be pleasing or displeasing to the lowly Galilean who "went about doing good?" Think of it, ye who would be his followers!

In a money way this measure would immediately improve the condition of the laboring man more than all the strikes and all the boycotts ever have improved it or ever can improve it. It would bring a thousand-fold more benefit than laboring men have ever asked for, sought for, or thought of. Intelligence and efficiency, and consequently comfort, would become the heritage of the poor. This measure would substantially bring about the abolishment of poverty.

This measure would settle all race questions by making the colored people intelligent and efficient workers. Each individual colored man and woman who becomes intelligent and efficient solves the race question as to himself or herself. John H. Alexander, the colored youth who stood second in his class at West Point this year, has solved the race question for himself. "I expect," he says, "to receive a second lieutenancy in the Ninth Cavalry, where there are colored men. I had not the slightest insult offered me at West Point on account of my color. Indeed, I think I was more leniently treated by my classmates than some white men. I minded my own business, and got along very well."

XXXII.

There is not a man, woman, or child in the country that would fail to reap benefit from this measure. The man who works for wages would have better wages. Taking all the young people under twenty out of the competition as wage-workers would necessarily cause wages to rise. In any country new employments are devised in proportion to the intelligence and skill of the people. Indians, Spaniards, and Turks, because they are unlettered and unskilful, never develop new employments. Americans, because they are intelligent and skilful, devise new employments constantly. Raising the intelligence and skill of this people in the manner proposed would develop endless new employments to the immense advantage of everybody.

And if the man who works for wages would have better wages, the man who has things to sell would have better customers. The higher men rise in intelligence and skill, the more they earn and the more they are able to buy. Every man who has things to sell is interested in having the position of the laboring man improved. Commerce thrives, not on tramps, but on well-to-do customers. The position of a merchant who wishes a general reduction of wages is the position of a man who wishes to impoverish his customers. No man of sense would wish to impoverish his own customers.

XXXIII.

This measure would benefit the farmer and the man in active business as much as it would the mere wage-earner. There would be a better market for beef and potatoes, for groceries, for dry goods, for boots and shoes. The preacher and the doctor and the dentist would fare better. Everybody would fare better by reason of the immense amount of money that would be put into circulation. With the impetus that would be given to business by this measure, after paying ten per cent tax on a million the remaining nine hundred thousand dollars would bring in more income every year than the original million would have done.

The immense amount of money which this measure would put in circulation would go into the hands of people who have little and are compelled to spend nearly all they have. As fast as collected it would go into circulation and make business brisk. Give a million of dollars to Mr. Jay Gould, and it enables him to corner more things. But divide a million dollars among ten thousand families, and it goes into circulation for the necessaries of life, and improves business. The laboring-man would profit much, the business man would profit still more, and the rising generation would profit most of all. Peace and prosperity would settle down among us forevermore, and they would be cheaply bought.

Nobody need be afraid to have the condition of the average man improved. Nobody will be the worse for it. Everybody will be the better for it. In the improvement of the condition of the common average man lies the hope of the world. This proposition does not mean that those who are up shall be dragged down ; it means that those who are down shall be helped up. It means not fewer, but more, ladies and gentlemen to the acre.

If all the people were educated as I propose, who would do the coarse drudgery? It will be a long time before the world will be without multitudes fit for nothing but drudgery. The people with ability for nothing else but coarse drudgery would do it. The people who could find nothing better to do would do it. The world is full of such people now, and I fear it will always be full of people who will be glad enough to do the drudgery. Who shaves you? Who shoulders your trunk? Rarely men of American birth, because they find ways of earning a livelihood more in accordance with their tastes. But barbers and porters abound everywhere; and if a thousand times as many were needed, Germany would easily furnish the barbers, and Ireland the porters.

XXXIV.

The American method of righting things is by argument and by the ballot. It presupposes an intelligent population. The education which did very well a hundred years ago is not sufficient for us now. The facts upon which intelligence must act are much more numerous, and they are increasing every day. Our affairs are a thousand-fold more complicated now than they were then.

In view of the difficulties which ignorance brings upon us, some would limit the right of suffrage to those who can read and write — as if those who can barely read and write are fit to have a voice in this government. The American remedy for ignorance is not a curtailment of rights and privileges. The true remedy for ignorance is to do away with it. The true remedy for ignorance is to provide high and broad education for all the people. The American remedy for ignorance is not a curtailment of rights and privileges, but an enlargement of intelligence.

Nineteen out of twenty American children begin the struggle of life without money.

With the manual training school education, they would be far better fitted to begin life without assistance than if they had been educated at Harvard or at Yale, because their acquaintance with things would be greater.

The proposition which I have stated is to give to the son of Mr. Vanderbilt's brakeman an education as good for all practical purposes as Mr. Vanderbilt can give to his own son. The proposition means brains to the front, no matter where they may be found.

The American idea is not to level men down to equality. The American idea is by means of intelligence to raise men up to equality. The carrying out of this proposition would be a greater step forward than has ever been taken towards giving all men a fair and equal start in the world — towards a fair field for all and favor to none — towards practical human equality. The proposed measure is the necessary and logical sequence of the immortal Declaration of our Revolutionary forefathers.

The American people educated in the manner proposed would be a people of intelligence and efficiency such as the world has never yet seen. Only the very few would be ignorant and inefficient. The many would be intelligent and efficient. This measure once enacted, all anxiety about the perpetuity of republican institutions would immediately cease. "The true principle of free and popular government," said Daniel Webster in his Plymouth Rock oration, "would seem to be so to construct it as to give to all, or at least to a very great majority, an interest in its preservation; to found it, as other things are founded, on men's interests. . . . The freest government, if it could exist, would not be long acceptable if the tendency of the laws were to create a rapid accumulation of property in a few hands, and to render the great mass of the population penniless."

XXXV.

Is there any danger in this proposition? Do high-school graduates riot? Is there any danger in general intelligence and general efficiency? Is there anything unfair in this proposition? Is it a scheme for the benefit of the few?

Would the nation get an equivalent for the money spent? In return for the money spent the nation would get intelligent and efficient citizens, who, instead of waiting for something to turn up, would be able to turn up something for themselves. The proposed measure means a population sufficiently intelligent and efficient to devise such legislation as shall put an end to the reign of the stock waterers. The proposed measure means that hereafter it shall be easier than now to acquire a competency by honest industry, — all the more because it will be made more difficult to acquire millions by stupendous confidence games. It means fewer millions acquired by cruising close up under the walls of the penitentiary, fewer penitentiary millionnaires, fewer tramps, fewer paupers, fewer hovels, and a larger number of comfortable people.

It will be said that such application of public money is contrary to usage. Since when have we in this country begun to object to things because they are new? Everything American is new. To govern by keeping men down is old. To govern by raising men up is new. Here, where everything is new, newness is not fatal. The only question that is to the point in this matter is, Is the proposition based upon common-sense? This is is the one blessed land under the sun in which one man with common-sense on his side is an eventual majority.

But, says some objector, all Europe would pour in upon us to get the benefit of such a state of things. That would be nothing new. All Europe is pouring in upon us now. If immigration is undesirable and dangerous, we would do better to begin to do something about it immediately. Half a million of immigrants have already landed in this country this year, and before the year is out the number will run up to nearly a million. These people are coming here by reason of the superior chances in life already offered them. They are coming lured by better wages for the grown people and the common school for the children. They are coming because at the very ends of the earth, the lowest of the low, the commonest of the common, and the humblest of the humble have heard and believe and know that here among utter strangers they will be safer from want and starvation than in their native places among friends. They are coming because they have heard and believe and know that here we feed the hungry, clothe the naked, give land to the landless and homes to the homeless. They are coming because heretofore we have taken from their dark dungeons the dazed victims of oppression and set them in the sunshine and fresh air of American liberty. They are coming because they have heard and believe and know that heretofore we have given so fair a field to all that the sons of European peasants, with a thousand generations of hewers of wood and drawers of water behind them, have here become chiefs. From his native bog and into the steerage, out of the steerage and through the Castle Garden of his day, in rags and tatters, carrying all his earthly belongings in a pocket handkerchief on a shillelah, came the Irishman, whose son, Andrew Jackson, became the hero of New

Orleans and President of the United States. If this immigration is undesirable and dangerous it is undesirable and dangerous now, and something should immediately be done to stop it. But if this immigration is undesirable and dangerous now, the measure I propose would "out of this nettle danger pluck the flower safety," by educating and Americanizing the children of the immigrants. With or without additional inducements these people will continue to come. Meanwhile we are surely not to cease taking measures for our own betterment lest by reason thereof a greater number should come. If we do not want them, let us say so, and put an end to their coming.

XXXVI.

To whom would this measure bring suffering? To no one. The only objection to it, then, is that, like the school tax which is levied for the good of all, this measure would deprive the few of what they could well spare, — spare without suffering and spare with profit, because it would be found to be a good investment. Socialism proposes that all production and all distribution shall be done by the State, — the State to direct everything and everybody; people are to eat what is set before them, wear what is issued to them, and do the tasks assigned them. High training for all would cultivate and intensify individual bias, and render odious the bare thought of Socialism. Communism proposes that no individual shall own anything, the community everything. In proposing a plan whereby all may be made more efficient and thereby more able to acquire property, have I not proposed a state of things which would be the very reverse of Communism? In showing how individual helplessness may be abolished, have I not proposed the very thing that would cause all agitation for communism to die out?

Some wiseacre will be sure to say that this proposition is communistic. This proposition is precisely as communistic as it is — and no more communistic than it is — to tax the man who has no children, in order to pay for the education of other people's children. Nearly all my life, having no children of my own, I have been made to pay taxes to educate other people's children. If this is communism, I approve of it. The school tax is levied to render more secure person, liberty, and property. The measure I propose is simply an additional means to accomplish the same end.

Our school system is the national insurance company which insures us against lawlessness and anarchy. The school tax is the annual insurance premium. What I propose is to strengthen the national insurance company and to lessen the dangers against which it insures. If the school tax is communistic, then this proposition is communistic. If the school tax is not communistic, then this proposition is not communistic. If this proposition is communistic, then the proposition of the national Republican platform of 1884 must have a strong leaning towards communism. It says : —

"We favor a wise and judicious system of general education by adequate appropriation from the national revenues, wherever the same is needed."

There is no communism in the national Republican platform of 1884. Neither is there any communism in my proposition. My proposition has nothing in common with communism. Communism might solve the capital and labor problem for a week, or a month, or a year, and then we should have the same problem back again. What we need, to solve the problem, is not a communistic distribution of property, which would not do it ; but what we must have, to solve the capital and labor problem effectually and permanently, is the greatest possible distribution of individual power and individual ability to acquire property. The greater the number of men who have property of their own, the smaller will be the number of men who will wish to divide things.

XXXVII.

This thing can be done by votes. It depends only upon ourselves. If we choose to take this thing in hand we can accomplish it, and we can accomplish it immediately. We are our own masters. This thing can be done locally, in each State separately. Any State Legislature can pass the necessary law, or if need be can pass and submit to the people of the State a constitutional amendment to carry into effect this measure.

In this movement the laboring-men of the city would have the sympathy and co-operation of the laboring-men of the country. The wage-workers of the city are not the only people interested in improving their own condition. The millions of American farmers will be as heartily for this measure as the wage-workers of the city. The proceeds of the tax would come mainly from the cities where the large fortunes are, and would in part flow out to the country, and give the country boys and girls an education and opportunities in life such as they have never yet had. The farmer who raises corn, eats coarse food, wears coarse clothes, and toils without ceasing for the lowest reward in this country, will be in favor of a measure which would give his children opportunities in the world equal with those of the broker who sells corn when he has none, and buys corn when he wants none, and thereby gets money wherewith to clothe himself and his wife and his children in purple and fine linen and to fare sumptuously every day. It will be the farmer's very first chance to begin to get anywhere near even with the transporters and leeches who impoverish him and literally make him work for them. For thousands of years has been asked the question which the writer of Ecclesiasticus puts: "How can he get wisdom that holdeth the plow, that glorieth in the goad, that driveth oxen and is occupied with the care of bullocks?" Never before has the question been answered, but it is answered by the Manual Training School and the measure which I advocate. A struggle for higher intelligence and efficiency would command the sympathy of the whole American people as nothing else would. The succession tax, and, by means of it, higher intelligence and efficiency for the people, would as a platform fire the land with enthusiasm.

XXXVIII.

Does the magnitude of the work appall? Are we, the people, to be afraid of a great undertaking? Are we not the same people who, only a few years ago, in a great cause, raised and kept on foot a million of men, at an expense of several millions of dollars each day? Are we not the same people who have nearly paid the national debt? On all the earth no other nation has ever done the like.

On all the earth there has never been a higher aspiration for a people. On all the earth no other nation has ever set itself so high an aim. The proposition is that here and now, in our generation and upon our soil, shall begin to come to pass that better condition for mankind whereof in their raptures poets have dreamed, for which in their agonies saints have prayed, for which upon the world's battlefields patriots have fought and bled and died.

When upon this soil was born the first child of our race, the genius of America stood by the humble cradle and said: Unto you and your children forevermore do I give this noble land. It is a land unequalled for resources; manifold and plentiful shall be the harvests. There shall be enough and to spare for all, full measure, shaken down and running over. Hitherto the world has been full of strong government and weak people. In this land, in schools free for all, shall be taught ideas clear as diamonds and broad as the universe. Intelligence shall make the people strong, the people shall be the government, and the strength of the people shall be the strength of the government. There shall be a fair field for all, and favor for none. By doing noble deeds each man shall here at pleasure write his own patent of nobility. The sweetest lay of the poet, the cunningest strain of the musician, and the never-ending note of the trumpet of fame shall be for the child of the humblest cottage.

THE MANUAL TRAINING SCHOOL.

A man should have a farm or a mechanical craft for his *culture*. — R. W. EMERSON.

Let the youth once learn to take a straight shaving off a plank, or draw a fine curve without faltering, or lay a brick level in its mortar, and he has learned a multitude of other matters which no lips of man could ever teach him. — JOHN RUSKIN.

The great question of the world is how to give every man a man's share in what goes on in life. Not a pig's share, nor a horse's share, not the share of a machine fed with oil only to make it work, and nothing else. It is n't a man's share just to mind your pin-making, and higgle about your own wages, and bring up your family to be ignorant sons of ignorant fathers, and no better prospect; that is a slave's share. — GEORGE ELIOT.

If we ask a boy to take his place at a carpenter's bench, it is not that we wish to make a carpenter of him, but that we wish to make him more of a man. We know that there is only one chance in fifty that he will use the saw, the chisel, the plane, the hammer, as the tools by which he earns his bread; but if he has had proper training in their use, he will carry to his work in life, whatever it may be, not only a better hand and a better eye, but also a better mind, a mind more perfectly filled and rounded out on all sides. — FRANCIS A. WALKER.

MANUAL TRAINING SCHOOL.

I.

YANKEE ingenuity is proverbial. The Yankee was made ingenious by the adverse circumstances under which he existed. The main circumstance which made the Yankee ingenious was that whenever he wanted anything he himself had to make it or go without it. As the Yankee wanted a great many things he learned to make a great many things, and thus he became very ingenious. But adverse circumstances alone do not develope ingenuity. The North Carolinian has had adverse circumstances quite equal to those of the Yankee. Why has not he become ingenious? Simply, because with his adverse circumstances the North Carolinian has not had the spelling-book and the New-England primer to stir up a circulation in his head. The saving element in the Yankee's adverse circumstances, which has made him ingenious, and from the lack of which the North Carolinian has failed to become ingenious, is the Common School.

II.

The adverse circumstances under which each man had to make everything for himself have disappeared from this country. Instead of them has come the Manual Training School, which is a complete set of improved adverse Yankee circumstances for training the young in intelligence and ingenuity. The class which Professor Woodward of St. Louis graduated in 1883 introduced into the world an entirely new product. " Boys about eighteen years of age, who three years before had never touched tools with a view to becoming skilled with them, had drawn plans for several steam-engines. They had drawn the patterns on paper. They had made the patterns in wood. They had been forced to have the castings done by other hands, because there were in the school no facilities for making castings. They could have made the castings if there had been facilities for doing so. The boys had done the chipping and the filing and the lathe-work. They had put together their engines. They had connected them to a supply of steam, and at the word of command steam was turned on, and the engines began to run. In the education of these boys their purely mental studies had not been neglected." In the language of Mr. Dowd, the Superintendent of Schools at Toledo, all their manual exercises had been intellectual exercises, and they were ready to stand right up and be examined in books side by side with boys who had devoted all their time to books.[1]

[1] See Appendix, VI.

III.

At the present time the majority of children are taken away from school early in order to learn to gain their livelihood. Millions are thus kept in life-long ignorance. Parents take their children from school early now, not only to avoid the expense of keeping them there, but often because parents fail to see that more schooling would make their children better bread-winners. It is only reasonable to suppose that if the children could be taught at school more of that which would help them to gain their livelihood, parents would make far greater sacrifices than now to keep them there longer.

Our need is something which shall keep the children at school throughout the public course, including the high school. This want is, as I believe, to be supplied by the Manual Training School. The Manual Training School is simply a high school with the manual feature added. The manual feature can be added to any high school. From the experience we have already had, we know that the manual feature added to the high-school course will fill the high schools and necessitate their multiplication. The high schools are not full, but the manual training schools, in spite of high tuition fees, are full to overflowing. They are full of boys of whom at least one half would not have been in any school but for the manual training. When the curriculum of the manual training school, which embodies the production of superior bread-winning qualities, together with high mental training, shall in the public high school, free of charge, become the birthright of every child in the land, it will become clearer to all that more schooling will make better bread-winners. The bread-winning training will lure parents and children, and it will lure the children into superior intelligence. If the Manual Training School had no other justification, it would be amply justified by its tendency to keep boys at school till the age of seventeen or eighteen. Keeping the boys at school till that age would give us intelligent citizens. It would raise immensely the general intelligence of the people.

IV.

The late Secretary of the Interior, Mr. Teller, is reported to have said that if all the Indian children could have the moderate education which is given to only a few of them at Carlisle Barracks there would never be another Indian war. Leaving out of view all considerations of humanity, how much cheaper it would be to educate the Indians than it is to shoot them. It costs about $1,000 to train an Indian. It costs the lives of ten white men and thousands of dollars to shoot one.

If all the Mormon children could have a complete high-school education there would soon be an end of polygamous Mormonism. Do you think the graduates of a high school would become plural wives? Polygamy is possible only with extremely ignorant women. Rarely do any but the the most ignorant women found in this country become Mormons, and Mormonism is recruited most readily from European peasant women, because to them even the polygamy of Utah is a promotion.

If all the children in the land could have a complete high-school education there would be far less drunkenness than there is. The average man drinks in proportion to his ignorance. The savage drinks all he can get. In drinking, the ignorant man in civilized life follows closely upon the heels of the savage. Intelligence develops tastes for better things, which conquer the brutal appetite for strong drink.

This is a government by school-masters. If we had fewer school-masters we should be forced to have more policemen and more soldiers. It is wiser, safer, better, and cheaper to train good citizens than it is to shoot bad ones.

V.

Benjamin Franklin said: "Empty your purse into your head; then you can never lose your money, and you will always be sure of a high rate of interest."

Thomas Jefferson said: "If a nation expects to be ignorant and free in a state of civilization, it expects what never was and never will be."

"Promote," said George Washington, "as an object of prime importance, institutions for the general diffusion of knowledge."

I firmly believe that the American people are ready to support a higher education. To do it is the interest of everybody. Commerce and industry profit by every step in the elevation of man. Where men are ignorant and unskilled there is no commerce. The savage is not commercial. He is a poor customer. He has nothing to sell, and therefore he can buy nothing. The unskilled ignorant laborer in a civilized country is likewise a poor customer. He can earn but little, and therefore he can buy but little. The higher men rise in skill and intelligence, the better customers they are. With every step in the elevation of man commerce and industry increase. Commerce and industry therefore favor the highest possible elevation of all men.

VI.

The Manual Training School teaches no particular trade. It teaches the rudiments of all the trades. At first blush it would seem impossible to teach a boy in three years, two hours each school-day, the rudiments of all the trades. The difficulty is smaller than it seems. There are only seven hand tools: the axe, the saw, the plane, the hammer, the square, the chisel, and the file. The graduate of a manual training school has not learned a particular trade, but he is within from one to three months of knowing, quite as thoroughly as an apprentice who has served years, any one of twenty trades to which he may choose to turn. Having learned the use of all the tools, he can easily turn to any modification of them which he may need in any employment. He is a superior draughtsman. He has an intelligence far beyond that of the average artisan, and the three years' apprentice is in no wise to be compared with him. If thrown out of one employment by the invention of a machine, the graduate of a manual training school can easily turn to any other employment. The boy who has learned the use of all the tools has found out his bias, if he has any, and he can then go in the direction in which he is at his best. He need not go all through life working at a trade for which he is ill-fitted. The intelligence and diversity of skill acquired in the manual training school make the boy a superior workman in any employment.

VII.

The apprentice system was the old method for training skilled artisans, but steam has put an end to it. In a shop where steam is used it costs too much to make the wheels go round to permit an unskilled apprentice to use the tools. Nobody but a skilled workman can be permitted to use the money-eating tools driven by steam. Steam has killed the apprentice system. There is no place where an American boy can learn a trade except the penitentiary.

The Manual Training School fills the place of the apprentice system. It much more than fills the place. It fills the place of the apprentice system as the locomotive fills the place of the stage-coach. In other words, the Manual Training School fills the place of the apprentice system a thousand times over. The apprentice in a shop is a hewer of wood and a drawer of water, the last and least important individual in the shop. In the Manual Training School, on the contrary, the boy is the most important individual. He is the object for which the school exists. He is the material that is to be finished. Instead of being left to himself to pick up what he can, competent and intelligent instructors devote themselves to his training. The boy, as an apprentice, exists for the benefit of the shop. When the boy is a scholar in a manual training school, the shop exists for his benefit.

VIII.

Mr. Foley, who was for many years an instructor of forging, vise-work and machine-tool-work in the Boston Mechanic Art School, before becoming an instructor had served an apprenticeship of seven years, and had worked at his trade for several years. Mr. Foley has seen and tried both methods and knows whereof he speaks. He says: "It appears like throwing away two or three years of one's life to spend them in attaining a knowledge of a business that can be acquired by a proper course of instruction in sixty days, two hours each day. The dexterity that comes from practice can be reached as quickly after the one hundred and twenty hours' instruction as after two or more years spent as an apprentice under the adverse circumstances of ordinary apprenticeship."

The wonder is, not that boys so quickly learn the use of tools in a manual training school under competent instructors, but seeing how easily they learn, the wonder is that anybody should ever have undertaken to learn the use of tools in any other way.

The Manual Training School has come, and it has come to stay. For purposes both of education and of industry we shall abandon the manual training school method when we abandon the locomotive and go back to the stage coach.

IX.

The drudgery of the apprentice tends to stupefy him. All work and no play makes Jack a dull boy. While the manual training requires as close attention as any study, it is nevertheless so complete a change from studying a book that in the midst of study it is in the nature of diversion and recreation. Was there ever a boy who did not delight in tools? Last year the boys in the Chicago Manual Training School asked for a holiday Washington's birthday, and having obtained it, they immediately asked for permission to spend their holiday in the carpenter-shop of the school.

Of course nothing can make a bright boy out of a dull boy, but there are bright boys not easily kept down to study who gladly swallow the bitter pill of study by reason of the delight which they take in the manual training. The editor-in-chief of one of the St. Louis daily papers told me some time ago that he had never been able to keep his boy in any school until he sent him to the St. Louis Manual Training School, but that now the boy cannot be kept away, and wishes that school kept Saturday and Sunday. It may be said with truth, both of bright boys and of dull boys, that the Manual Training School has a wider reach of allurement for their faculties than any other school hitherto known.

X.

There are people who are afraid that if a boy learns the use of tools he must necessarily be a mechanic, and can never rise in the world. The very first condition for rising in the world is knowledge of some sort. Many men are kept down in the world by ignorance and want of skill, but I have never yet seen any man or heard of any man who was kept down by knowledge and skill.

We are asked, "Shall we train five hundred thousand mechanics where only fifty thousand can find employment?" The answer is, that the education of the Manual Training School is not a mere training of mechanics. The Manual Training School educates boys, not to become mechanics, but to become men of intelligence and skill. It educates them so that they may have open to them a wider field of employment than they could have in any other way. It educates them so that they may have open to them all employments. Is there a farmer who would not be a better farmer with this training? Is there a physician who would not be a better physician with it? Is there a lawyer who would not be a better lawyer with it? Is there any man, rich or poor, engaged in any pursuit to whom this training would not be an advantage? The education of the Manual Training School will be just as serviceable for the four hundred and fifty thousand scholars who are not to be mechanics as it will be for the fifty thousand who are to be mechanics.

XI.

We are told that in our education we must emphasize the man and not the mechanic. Which plan puts the greater emphasis on the man, — the plan which educates the young only by means of books, or the plan which gives them an equal knowledge of books and a wide range of practical skill besides?

We are told that the practical education is not of the hand to skill, but of the brain to directive intelligence. Which plan is likely to produce the greater degree of intelligence, — the plan under the operation of which the children drop out of school at the age of ten or twelve, only a very few reaching the high school, or the manual training plan, which would keep the children at school through all the grades, and get them into and through the high school? Manual training never means less education or less intelligence. Manual training always means more education and more intelligence.

XII.

The skill acquired in the Manual Training School is so valuable that it is not necessary to show that the mental progress of the scholar is as great as if he devoted all his time to books. But those who should know say that the mental progress is as great as if all the time were devoted to the study of books. There is nothing absurd in supposing that four and a half hours of mental work and two hours of manual training may produce quite as good mental results as six and a half hours of continuous book study. Surely no one will question that the mental training must help the manual training. I see as little reason to doubt that the manual may help the mental training. In the manual training school there is not a word spoken or a thing done except with a view to education. Mr. Goss, of Purdue University, Indiana, well says that manual training is mental training by hand practice. He says that he considers an hour in the shop as valuable for intellectual training as an hour of book study, and two hours in the shop as valuable as two hours of study.

XIII.

Dr. Belfield, of the Chicago Manual Training School, says: "My opinion is that an hour in the shop of a well-conducted manual training school develops as much mental strength as an hour devoted to Virgil or Legendre. I am satisfied that three years of a manual training school will give at least as much purely intellectual growth as three years in the ordinary high school, because every school-hour, whether spent in the class-room, the drawing-room, or the shop, is an hour devoted to intellectual training. I am convinced that the manual training school boy's comprehension of some essential branches of knowledge will be as far superior to that of the ordinary high school boy's as the realization of the grandeur and beauty of the Alps to the man who has seen their glories is superior to the conception of him who has merely read of them."

Professor Woodward, of the St. Louis Manual Training School, who has had thirteen years' experience, says substantially the same thing.

The testimony of all teachers who have had experience in manual training is to the same effect. Pestalozzi, Fröbel, and their thousands of followers, and the teachers of the thousands of Slöjd Schools in Sweden and Finland all tell the same story.

What manual training teachers say is that well on this side of the point where weariness begins manual training is equal to books for producing mental growth. In a manual training lesson of two hours the average boy of fourteen keeps up a lively interest. Three hours would probably fatigue him. Carried beyond the point up to which a lively interest can be maintained, a lesson in manual training is like any other lesson given to a fatigued scholar, — a mere waste of time.

XIV.

The wealth of a nation depends upon its skill. Before the invention of canoes, fishing nets, bows and arrows, savages are uncomfortably and pitiably poor. Without tools with which to get food they are always liable to starve. With the invention of canoes and nets, fishing gives them food and lessens their liability to starve. With the invention of bows and arrows, hunting gives them food, and with a little agriculture in addition they become reasonably secure from starvation. Thus human comfort depends upon human skill. A nation with little skill is poor. A nation with great skill is rich. Steam is the principal tool of modern times, and the nations are getting rich in proportion to their skill in using it. England is the foremost nation for skill in using steam, and England is the foremost nation in acquiring wealth. We are next to England for skill in using steam, and we are next to England in getting rich. There are only sixty millions of us, but steam does the work of probably two hundred millions more. The result is an increase of wealth within our borders such as the world has never before seen.

A Spaniard or a Turk has only one pair of hands for producing things. By means of steam an Englishman has industrially ten pairs of hands. An American in like manner has ten pairs of hands. Eventually skill and intelligence will bring us for every man a hundred pairs instead of ten pairs of hands. Increase of skill is worth struggling for. Every advance in skill increases the comfort of every man, woman, and child in the country.

XV.

A hundred years ago nineteen out of every twenty men in this country were farmers. The proportion of farmers to the whole population has decreased every day since; it is now decreasing every day. The proportion of men engaged in the industrial arts has increased correspondingly, and is now increasing every day.

As improvements multiply in agricultural machinery, a greater number of men can go into industrial pursuits and still leave the supply of food ample. The McCormick reaper alone has liberated from farming millions of men. There is only just so much use for agricultural products. When a man has had enough bread he does not wish any more. Enough is enough. Industrial products, on the contrary, are unlike bread, of which enough is enough. Of industrial products we want all those that we know of, we want all those that we have heard of, and we want all those that we have never seen and never heard of as fast as they can be invented. Alexander the Great never craved a fine watch, simply because watches were not then in existence. Had they existed, Alexander would have wanted the very best watch that could be made. Our great-grandmothers never felt the need of sewing-machines, simply because to them sewing-machines were inconceivable. Thirty years ago we never thought of riding in sleeping-cars, because there were none. A valuable invention, as soon as it is known, becomes an article of pressing necessity. We can never get a sufficient variety of industrial products. Our industrial wants are bounded only by the limits to human invention.

XVI.

The destinies of the ancient world were moulded by soldiers and war. The ancient world came to an end and the modern world began with the steam-engine. The destinies of the modern world are moulded by mechanics and machinery. Our nation of sixty millions is the offspring of the steam-engine. Only by means of steam could the many millions have been carried across the Atlantic and scattered all over the land.

The representative man of the ancient world was the proud, fierce warrior, steel-clad, sabred, booted, and spurred, who made of the average man a cripple or a corpse. The representative man of to-day is the fustian-clad, humble, greasy mechanic, who makes this a comfortable world to live in. To the proud warrior belongs the dead past, with all its exploded stupidities. To the humble artisan belongs the great future, with all the hopes of humanity. The humble artisan will yet invent a machine that shall do all the work of the world while he sits by with his hand on the valve reading his newspaper.

XVII.

Skill with small intelligence increases very slowly. Skill coupled with great intelligence, like any other large capital, increases very rapidly. A century makes very little difference in the skill of a tribe of Indians. Their intelligence is too limited. But look at the amazing increase of our skill during the last hundred years. What an increase of skill there would be if henceforth all the children could be educated in manual training schools! During our war no man of sense wanted one of our armies to be commanded by a volunteer. From first to last, on both sides, the West-Pointers stood at the head. What West Point is to the army, the Manual Training School will become to industry, — and more, because it will train not only the officers of industry, but likewise the rank and file. When this shall come to pass there will be no more tariff agitation in this country, because the skill developed will of itself forever put an end to all foreign competition upon American soil.

XVIII.

Am I over-stating the effect upon industry of manual training? It cannot be overstated. Thirty years ago the French bought all their cotton goods in England. They then bought English machinery, brought over English workmen to run it, established a training school for the cotton industry at Mülhouse, and now the finest cotton goods used in England and in this country are made in France. To sixpence worth of cotton the French add so much skilled labor that we pay them a dollar for it. They buy of us the raw material, and sell us back the finished product. To use the time-honored illustration, they buy of us the hide for a sixpence and sell us back the tail for a shilling. In like manner has France obtained control of her own market for watches by establishing schools for the watch industry at Besançon and elsewhere. There are trade schools in every large city of France; nearly every industry has its special schools; and these schools are increasing, not only in France, but all over Europe. In fact, within the last ten years the Germans have been gaining upon the French by means of technical schools.

XIX.

The Manual Training School reverses the cry that to compete in the markets of the world our labor must come down. The Manual Training School says, on the contrary, that workingmen must go up higher. The meaning and intention of the Manual Training School movement are that workingmen shall become more intelligent, more skilful, do better work, and earn more money. The Manual Training School preaches the gospel of the blue ribbon. Mr. Perrot, of Switzerland, came to this country in 1876 to exhibit his machinery for making watches. Landing in New York, he hastened to Philadelphia to secure a place to show his wares. He was assigned space next to that of the Waltham Watch Company. He took just one look at the Waltham machinery, and then he telegraphed to his agent in New York not to permit his own machinery to be landed, but to send it back to Europe by the ship in which it had come. In the autumn Mr. Perrot went back to Switzerland and told his countrymen that American workmen earned three times as much as Swiss workmen, but that by reason of the intelligence and skill of American workmen, they were well worth their triple wages, and that, high as were their wages, Switzerland could never again hope to sell watches in the American market. We could not, if we would, compete in making labor come down. Europe can easily beat us at that. The downward competition is not open to us. I hope we shall never try to enter upon it. But with its despotisms and its armies, its debts and its ignorance, Europe has no chance in the upward competition. We can, if we will, raise the intelligence and skill of American workingmen, so that our industries shall be above all competition. For a nation, as well as for an individual, there is always room higher up.

XX.

Some time ago one of my friends told me of a mill in New England which made muslin selling at twelve cents a yard. By making it of a checkered pattern at an infinitesimally additional expense it sold quite as readily for twenty-two cents. At twelve cents the plain muslin had to compete with the plain muslin of the whole world. With a little originality of design added, it stood alone, by itself, without competition. "What do you mix with your colors?" was asked of the painter. "Brains," said the master, "brains." The more brains we mix with our industry the better it pays. Industry pays just in proportion as it is mixed with brains.

Our industries are waiting for more skill. They are willing to pay and they can afford to pay any reasonable price for it. A few years ago we made in this country scarcely any carpets; now we make so many carpets that we import scarcely any. But we still buy abroad the higher grades of carpets. The carpet industry fails as yet in originality of design and the higher grade of workmanship. Within the last five years the silk industry has tripled in this country. But we still buy abroad the higher grades of silk. Both the carpet and the silk industries are waiting for the designers and fine workmen who do not yet exist, but whom the Manual Training School must start on their career.

XXI.

The advantage in diversified employments is like the advantage there is in not carrying all one's eggs in one basket. Skill breeds diversity of employment, and the more diversity of employment there is, the fewer will there be of strikes and lockouts. If the men who are now engaged in making carpets and silks were still engaged in making cotton cloth, there would be an immediate overproduction of cotton cloth and a strike and a lockout. The Manual Training School creates skill. Skill increases and multiplies and produces diversity of employment. Diversity of employment prevents strikes and lockouts. The Manual Training School does not train mere mechanics. The mere mechanic is a man with only one skill. Any day a machine may come and do the only thing he can do. When the mechanic's one employment fails him he is helpless. Not so with the boy educated in the Manual Training School. Helplessness is not in his vocabulary. He has learned to think and he has learned to put his thoughts into things. His brain has learned to plan, and his hands have learned to do what his brain plans. He has learned that things will yield, and he has learned how to make them yield. His intelligence and his skill fill him with power. He has acquired so much power that he will be his own master. He will never need to strike, and he will never be locked out. Of the kind who strike and who can be locked out, there are always too many in the world. Of the manual training school boy's kind there are never enough. By applying his brains and his eyes and his hands to books, to tools, to wood and to iron, he has mastered the great lesson of power.

XXII.

So far as human problems are solvable, they are solvable by intelligence and skill. One thousand manual training schools in the land would not only do away with strikes and lockouts, but they would solve the whole capital and labor problem. "Communism might solve the capital and labor question for a week or a month or a year and then we should have the same problem back again. But the Manual Training Schools would solve the capital and labor problem permanently by doing away with it. For the boys educated in the Manual Training School there will be no capital and labor problem. Wherever they go they will be able to achieve for themselves their due share of the good things of this world. What we need to solve the problem, is not a communistic distribution of property, which would not do it; but what we must have to solve the capital and labor problem effectually and permanently is the greatest possible distribution of individual power and individual ability to acquire property. The greater the number of men who have property of their own, the smaller will be the number of men who will wish to divide things."

XXIII.

It is said that we cannot have manual training in the high school until we can offer equal advantages to boys and girls. If it were the rule in this world, that nobody is to be comfortable until everybody can be comfortable, nobody would ever be comfortable. The Manual Training School will eventually be as serviceable for girls as it is for boys. I think it will be thus serviceable for girls the very moment manual training is put into the high school. Women wisely do not always choose to stay within the limits men make for them. Being themselves chiefly interested, they prefer to try things for themselves. In Paris many women are now studying architecture. Many girls will be glad to avail themselves of all the instruction in drawing in the Manual Training School, and for their benefit the course in drawing may be extended. Many girls will undertake the course in wood-work as it is now, and for their benefit wood-carving may be immediately introduced. Nor must we forget that the average woman marries a man. Women have every reason to wish that the average man may become more intelligent, more skilful, and more efficient. The women who are not to marry and who have their own way to make in the world have every reason to wish that the boys now growing up may qualify themselves for more virile employments than those of dry-goods clerks, notaries public, bookkeepers and the like, which should long ago have been in the hands of women. Men and women are equally interested in putting manual training into the high school.

XXIV.

Can we afford to give to all the education of the Manual Training School at public expense? Training the young is the best investment that can be made. Bring up a boy in a hovel in Ireland and he will grow up to come over here to dig and shovel at a dollar a day. His son, born in Chicago, takes in the spelling-book and some mechanical skill, and earns two dollars a day. The shoveller's grandson may go to the Chicago Manual Training School and thereafter earn from three to five dollars and upwards indefinitely, according to his capacity. The raw material capable of the greatest possible improvement is human raw material. The raw material that yields the greatest possible profit in being improved is human raw material. European nations spend millions in training their young men for war. We could well afford to spend equal millions in training our young men for peace. Rather than do without the intelligence and efficiency which manual training schools would bring us, we could well afford, not only to establish the schools at public expense, but we could afford besides to pay to every scholar in them a salary to support him, as we do to every cadet at West Point.

XXV.

The only objection that can be made to giving every child in the land the manual training school education is the expense. The answer to the objection of expense is that the education will bring us in return a hundred fold for every dollar we spend. Instead of impoverishing us, this education is precisely what will bring us wealth. When we come to understand how well it will pay in money to give every child the manual training school education, instead of doing it with reluctance, we shall do it with alacrity. This nation is in the very depths of poverty compared to what it would be if every child in the land were educated in the Manual Training School.

Stanley says that there are forty millions of people on the Congo, all of them naked and poor. He says that the country in which they live is one of endless natural wealth. In the midst of all this wealth, the Africans are in the depths of poverty, simply because they are ignorant.

This country, with all its immense resources was once in the complete possession of the

Indians. The Indians did not get rich. They were not even comfortable. They starved and froze to death, simply because they did not know anything. We took their inheritance and with what little we know, see what we have done.

It is not in what is in the earth, nor in the material things that are on the earth that the wealth of a nation lies. It is in the training of the brains of the people; it is in the intelligence of the people that the wealth of a nation lies.

XXVI.

Ignorance and discomfort go together. Intelligence and comfort go together. With increase of intelligence comes increase of comfort.

Only a few centuries ago nearly everybody was ignorant and nearly everybody was poor and uncomfortable. Only the very few were comfortable. Comfort was the exception. Hunger and nakedness were the rule. The sun shone then as brightly as it does now and the earth was as teeming and fruitful then as it is now. Our ancestors got less out of the earth than we do, because they knew less than we do. We get more out of the earth than they did, because we know more than they did.

The way comfort has increased with intelligence proves that there is in this world an abundance for all who are fitted to get their share. One reason that so many people are uncomfortable is that they are not fitted by their training to get their share of the good things of this world. With better training we should have a more comfortable world. With each step towards better training, we shall have a more comfortable world.

XXVII.

To leave the great mass of the people in ignorance is to leave them in hopeless poverty. To educate all is substantially to give equal opportunities to all. To educate all is to give comfort and prosperity to all.

The education of the Manual Training School, so eminently adapted to the young, no matter what they are to do in life, we must give to every child. Not only must the Manual Training School be open to every child, but every child must have the benefit of it. Heretofore in this country the aim has been to educate up to a certain point all the children. But the aim has been to give them as little education as the children could get along with. We must change this and give to every child all the education the child can take and all we know how to give.

If our American civilization means anything, it means that the time shall surely come when, no matter what it costs to educate him, no child shall be left to grow up in ignorance.

If our American civilization means anything over and above and distinct from other civilizations, it means that the earth and the good things of the earth are the heritage, not of the few, but of the many.

XXVIII.

To give to every child in the land the manual training school education is not as wild a scheme for us, considering our means, as it was for the puritan Pilgrims with their slender means to keep every child at school; and that is what they did when New England was yet a wilderness and in the depths of poverty. This is the law under which they did it: "Every township, after the Lord hath increased them to the number of fifty householders, shall appoint one to teach all the children to write and read; and when any town shall increase to the number of a hundred families, they shall set up a grammar-school." High above that of princes and kings and fighters of battles, towers the fame of those grim old Puritans, and forevermore it shall increase and grow brighter.

Green, the English historian, says that in the midst of the eighteenth century New England was the one part of the world where every man and woman was able to read and write. Has the common school of New England paid for itself? For answer look at the wealth of New England. If to-day the wealth of New England were in silver dollars, the silver dollars would almost outweigh the rocks of New England.

The advent of the Manual Training School marks an epoch in our history. Like the Common School, the Manual Training School is an institution which the many will not permit the few to appropriate. It has in it that which will not only make permanent the institutions we all love, but it has in it that which will eventually produce the American ideal,— a nation without an ignorant man and without a pauper.

XXIX.

The individual requires intelligence to hold his own in the world, and our government requires intelligence not only in the few but in the many. Having solved the problem of managing a State without a king at the top, we now find that the ignorant man at the bottom of the State is almost as much of a nuisance as was the king. We find that we are governed by the ignorant man quite as much as we are by the intelligent man; and rather more, because the ignorant man likes to govern us, and he is willing and can afford to devote all his time and attention to it.

Our problem is at all hazards to get rid of the ignorant man. The most ignorant man in the State has a vote that counts for as much as the vote of the most intelligent man. What the most intelligent man in the State wants to accomplish for the good of everybody cannot be done until a sufficient number of ignorant men are convinced that it will not hurt them; because not until they are convinced can a majority be got to vote for it.

As the strength of the chain is only equal to that of its weakest link, so the action of the government is constantly kept down towards the level of the most ignorant man in the State. I would not on that account deprive the ignorant man of his vote. Deprived of his vote he would be a man with a just grievance. In comparison with him, all the other people in the State would be a privileged class. No, I would not deprive the ignorant man of his vote. But I would so arrange things that his boys and girls should be sure to get the benefit of the Manual Training School. As to the ignorant man himself, eventually he would die, and under the circumstances his kind would die out.

XXX.

The great advantage of self-government for which it is to be prized above all others is that it is a government of peace. The rule of the people means peace. The many are for peace and against war, because upon them war piles all its burdens and all its sufferings. On the contrary where the few rule, the very air is always full of war. The explanation is easy enough. War benefits and aggrandizes the few at the expense of the many. Nobles and princes, kings and potentates want fleets, and armies, conquests and glory. Being able to do as we like, having our own affairs in our own hands, knowing that if we dance, we ourselves must pay the piper, we seek no conquests. We want no military glory. It is our aim to build up ourselves, not upon the ruins of other people's happiness, but by the peaceful, skilful, and intelligent use of what we already own and have within our own borders. Never before in the world has there been a nation at once so powerful and so peaceful as ours. What the average American wants is in peace and plenty to live and labor and love. That we prize the government which enables us to do this is not to be wondered at.

The distance which our political system is ahead of even that of England is measured by the fact that if the two millions of men who have just been enfranchised in England had been on the coast of New England in 1620, they would then and there have been enfranchised 266 years ago.

XXXI.

Before landing at Plymouth, the Pilgrims on the Mayflower, in order to avoid all possibility of lawlessness, entered into an agreement amongst themselves concerning the manner in which their settlement should be governed. In this agreement each man pledged himself to submission and obedience to the laws that should be made in pursuance of it. The agreement reads like this : —

"In the name of God, Amen : We, whose names are under written, the loyal subjects of our dread Sovereign, King James, having undertaken, for the glory of God and advancement of the Christian faith, and honor of our King and country, a voyage to plant the first colony in the Northern parts of Virginia, do, by these presents, solemnly and mutually, in the presence of God and one of another, covenant and combine ourselves together into a civic body politic, for our better ordering and preservation and furtherance of the ends aforesaid ; and by virtue hereof, to enact, constitute, and frame such just and equal laws, ordinances, acts, constitutions, and offices, from time to time, as shall be thought most convenient for the general good of the colony. Unto which we promise all due submission and obedience."

That agreement instituted a government of the people, by the people, and for the people. It was the beginning of self-government in this country. It was the beginning of self-government in the world.

There were forty-one men on board of the Mayflower, and forty-one men signed the agreement for self-government. No man was excluded because he was ignorant or because he was poor, or for any other reason whatever. That agreement is to-day the high-water mark of the world's statemanship. What Gladstone is doing in England now is only a feeble imitation of what the Pilgrims did on the Mayflower.

XXXII.

Self-government was easily possible for the forty-one men who landed on Plymouth Rock, because they were intelligent men. Had they been ignorant men self-government would have been full of difficulty for them. Ignorance becomes lawless and riots under circumstances under which intelligence discusses and convinces others, or is itself convinced and holds its peace. Ignorance is the arch enemy of self-government. If self-government is to flourish, ignorance must go. Self-government implies that as all men must rule, all men must be trained so as to be fit to rule. For its own preservation and perpetuation self-government requires the highest possible elevation of all men. What fresh air and food are to the human body the school and the printing-press are to self-government. Untrained brain power is wasted brain power, and self-government cannot afford to let brain power be wasted. Any boy on the street, when trained, may be a possible benefactor of his race. Any boy on the street, when educated, may be a possible General Grant.

Self-government requires that all the Abraham Lincolns be brought out of the Kentucky log-huts and set to stir the high chords in the nation's breast.

From Jamestown and Plymouth Rock down to the present moment the loftiest American thought is that in this country there shall be at the very earliest possible moment, free of charge for every child on the soil, the highest and best and most practical training the child can take and the world can give. The dream of commerce and industry is a land full of good customers. The dream of patriotism is a land full of free, intelligent and independent citizens. The dream of poesy is a land full of smiling, loving, happy homes. The dream of commerce and industry, the dream of patriotism, and the dream of poesy are all the same dream.

APPENDIX.

APPENDIX.

I.

From The Missouri Republican, January 1, 1887.

THE past year will be forever memorable as the year in which private armies of mercenary soldiers began to be established in this country. In Italy this would have been an old story; in America it is quite a new one. There for hundreds of years cities, nobles, prelates, merchant princes, and guilds of craftsmen, as well as sovereign States, found it expedient, and, as they thought, profitable, to have at their command and in their pay companies of armed men whose trade was war, and whose swords were ready to be drawn in any cause which promised them the best pay. Public right seemed to have no competent arbiter, and private war became inevitable. The sequel was what might have been expected. The blood of Italy was shed to exhaustion by the swords and stilettos of her own hired bravos; she became the easy prey of foreign foes, and fell into a state of degradation, which it took the pen of Gladstone to describe, in the good days of King Bomba. In this country it has been fondly supposed that public law was strong enough to do right and maintain right between the citizens of whom the commonwealth has jurisdiction. That, it now seems, was an error. When a difference occurs between a great pork-packer and his employees, it is not to the State that either party has resort; and to check apprehended violence the pork-packer finds it easier, and perhaps cheaper, to call out a regiment of hired soldiers, who have been armed and trained for the service of the highest bidder. We are by no means blaming Mr. Armour for hiring, nor Mr. Pinkerton for enlisting, such a regiment. We are simply pointing out that regiments of hired bravos are, in fact, openly enlisted, sold like Hessians, and sent into the field to serve whoever will pay best for them; that a system of private war has thus been openly inaugurated; and that the State seems to assume that it is all right.

There are always two sides in a war, whether it be a public or a private war; and in private wars, the experience of the world shows that when the one side has the advantage of wealth and power, the other seeks the advantages which may be had by means of secret conspiracies and murders. Tyranny has been tempered by assassination in many other countries than Russia, and in so-called republics as well as in autocracies. There was never a time in the history of mankind more full of danger than the present from secret combinations of men who think themselves wronged by powerful enemies. These are days when one man may become a terror to thousands. Dynamite and other chemicals well known to science can easily overcome any disparity of numbers, and the dread of it can make the lives of kings and kaisers burdensome, until they fall, like the present czar of all the Russias, into frenzies of terror and wild rage. All that is needed is absolute secrecy in the conspirators; and although the secrecy of numbers of men in any enterprise is all but impossible, yet the failure of one conspiracy after another never checks the spirit of conspiracy when it has taken hold of any class of men. The history of the Italian Carbonari and the Russian Nihilists is full of frightful significance. It was in vain that hundreds of thousands of the former were, and it is now in vain that hundreds of thousands of the latter continue to be, imprisoned, tortured, done to death in the most cruel ways of cruelty itself; the spirit of conspiracy is not repressed, — it spreads, and grows more cruel than its foe. What unimaginable irony it would be if, in this democratic country, the working class were to become infected with the spirit of conspiracy, so that the private armies of the capitalist were to be, not confronted, but circumvented and assassinated by invisible conspirators! Of this incomparably execrable spectacle the present year has seen more than some faint suggestions. The spirit of conspiracy is abroad among our people. Corporations conspire to rob us by systems of deliberate extortion; politicians conspire to compel one class of the people to pay taxes to another by ruinous imposts; the Anarchists of Chicago have learned that open murder is not safe for the murderers, but at the same time more than a million of workingmen have been learning the art of secret combination, — a lawful art, indeed, but one which lies only a step off from the arts of secret conspiracy.

It is idle to say that workingmen shall not combine for the protection of their interests, while Jay Gould and his confederates shall be free to combine at pleasure to make workingmen pay him and them, throughout this bitter winter, $2.50 per ton for coal more than the coal is worth, and that under penalty of starving to death. We can have no laws in this country which shall not at least pretend to be equal for all. If secret combinations of extortion are lawful on the one side, secret combinations are equally lawful to resist them on the other. And if private armies for the service of rich men are to be allowed, private armed conspiracies of other men will very soon make their appearance. What a spectacle of shame the whole thing is! What a confession to the world of the failure of our institutions! What a disgrace to the present state of our society! What a presage of the future of our country! Nothing will avert the threatening calamity but a stern resolve that no man nor combination of men shall usurp the functions of the State, and that neither Philip Armour nor Jay Gould, nor any society of men whatever, shall wage private war in free America.

But private war and dangerous combinations have at least a flavor of romance, and sometimes they have a pretext of justice, which blinds the eyes to their atrocity. The past year has developed something else which crawls with nothing but a spawn of filth. Private prisons have now been established under the control of private detectives who arrest men without warrant, confine them without let or hinderance, keep them in a torture chamber facetiously called a "sweat box," and carry them without question from city to city and from State to State; who procure their own incarceration with indicted criminals to worm confessions from them, or learn how to concoct false testimony to convict them; who, in short, usurp the place of law, defy the law, juggle with grand-juries, and laugh all rightful authority to scorn, until they choose to call upon the State to do their bidding. Have we, in good sooth, come to this, that lawful authority is so powerless and so contemptible that an unlawful procedure must be substituted for it in the hands of a paid volunteer of private individuals? If that is true, then we have entered on a revolution which will lead to worse things than the direst pessimist has yet dared to forebode. The whole condition of affairs as it is, and the worse condition into which we seem to be drifting, is simply appalling, and the question which will very speedily be solved is whether we are worthy of the heritage of law and liberty which was bought with blood by better men than we. If we are, the lessons of the past year will not fall unheeded. The people will be roused to that eternal vigilance which is the price of liberty, and loudly tell those whom it may concern that to usurp the functions of the State is high treason, and that the penalty of outraged sovereignty shall be death.

Extract from Editorial Article on " Pinkerton's Men," in The Nation, New York, Jan. 27, 1887.

It cannot be too soon or too well understood that, as an armed organization offering itself for hire for purposes of defence in various parts of the Union, Pinkerton's Men are, we must all admit, the greatest disgrace that has befallen the United States. No such evidence of our internal weakness and lawlessness as the existence and activity of this organization constitutes has been offered to the world since the present Government was founded. Its appearance in any other civilized country would fill to-day every man in it with shame and astonishment. For it is — let nobody shrink from this plain truth — an unmistakable sign of retrogression towards mediæval barbarism. Pinkerton is neither more nor less than the head of a band of mercenaries, such as each great landholder in the eleventh and twelfth centuries kept in his pay for the defence of his property and that of his vassals against the armed attacks of his neighbors. They are called into existence by exactly the same causes now as then,— the absence of a public force capable of enforcing the law of the land, and affording security for life and property to the peaceable and well-disposed. Now as then, now as at every time since the dawn of civilization, no men of the Aryan race who have accumulated property of any kind will submit to be despoiled of it, or interfered with in the management of it, or allow any person or body of persons to "go upon them or send upon them," as the Barons said in Magna Charta, without trying to defend themselves. If there are courts, they will appeal to the courts; if there are police, they will call in the police; if there are troops, they will ask for the troops to defend their rights under the law; but if neither courts, nor police, nor troops will do anything for them, they will hire an army of their own. Of course, this is anarchy in its first stage. The word is not a pleasant one, but it must be used when the occasion calls for it.

II.

THE following letter from Albert E. Macomber Esq., who is a member of the board of directors of the Toledo Manual Training School, explains itself: —

TOLEDO, Jan. 6, 1887.
MY DEAR COL. JACOBSON, —

Your note of the 4th inst. is at hand. I send you the last report, which contains about all there is to say about this department.

We secured last September a teacher from Mrs. Ewing's School in Iowa, — Miss Nellie E. Rawson. She is a bright young woman, a graduate of the Iowa State University, and thus comes to her work with no narrow preparation. She has three classes, of say sixteen each, — bright girls of the high-school age, who seem to be as full of enthusiasm for this instruction in practical cookery as the boys are in their line.

Last month the morning class invited the Board of Education and the Directors of the Manual Training School to a supper spread in the class-room, — everything on the tables having been prepared by the pupils; and the table and service did them great credit, and was a surprise to most of the guests.

Miss Rawson has been fully occupied with her classes in cooking, but next year a competent teacher will be secured to give instruction in garment-making. From our brief experience there seems no reason to doubt that the girls will take as kindly to this line of instruction as the boys do, in the shops, to their work. It was found that the majority of these bright girls were utterly ignorant of the first principles of practical household work, and it is evident that a School of Domestic Economy has just as wide a field of usefulness before it as the Manual Training School for Boys.

Very respectfully yours,

A. E. MACOMBER.

[*Toledo Manual Training School Catalogue*, 1887.]

COURSE OF COMBINED STUDY AND TRAINING FOR GIRLS.

DOMESTIC ECONOMY DEPARTMENT.

FIRST YEAR.

(1.) *Mathematics.* — Arithmetic.
(2.) *Science.* — Physical Geography.
(3.) *Language.* — Grammar, Spelling, Writing, English composition.
} Senior Grammar School.

(4.) *Drawing.* — Free Hand and Mechanical, Lettering.
(5.) *Domestic Economy.* — Care and use of tools, and how to handle them. Light Carpentry, Wood-Carving.
} Manual Training School.

SECOND YEAR.

(1.) *Mathematics.* — Algebra, Arithmetic.
(2.) *Science.* — Physiology and Botany.
(3.) *Language.* — Grammar, Rhetoric, Writing.
} Junior High School.

(4.) *Drawing.* — Free Hand and Mechanical. Designs for Wood-Carving. Clay-Modelling.
(5.) *Domestic Economy.* — Introduction to course in Cooking, or Garment Cutting and Making. Use of Household Tools. Light Shop-work.

} Manual Training School.

THIRD YEAR.

(1.) *Mathematics.* — Geometry, Arithmetic reviewed.
(2.) *Science.* — Physics.
(3.) *Language.* — English, Composition, History.
(4.) *Drawing.* — Free Hand and Architectural, Designing from Plant and Leaf Forms.

} Middle High School.

(5.) *Domestic Economy.* — Instruction in Preparing and Cooking Food, Purchasing Household Supplies, Care of the Sick, etc.

} Manual Training School.

FOURTH YEAR.

(1.) *Mathematics.* — Plane Trigonometry, Mechanics.
(2.) *Science.* — Chemistry, Book-keeping, Ethics; Rights and Duties, Laws of Right Conduct.
(3.) *Language.* — Political Economy, English Literature and Composition.

} Senior High School.

(4.) *Drawing.* — Machine and Architectural Details, Decorative Designing.
(5.) *Domestic Economy.* — Cutting, Making, and Fitting of Garments, Household Decorations, Typewriting, etc.

} Manual Training School.

The above course in Domestic Economy is arranged with special reference to giving young women such a liberal and practical education as will inspire them with a belief in the dignity and nobleness of an earnest womanhood, and incite them to a faithful performance of the every-day duties of life; it is based upon the assumption that a pleasant home is an essential element of broad culture, and one of the surest safeguards of morality and virtue.

The design of this course is to furnish thorough instructions in applied housekeeping and the sciences relating thereto, and students will receive practical drill in all branches of housework, in the purchase and care of family supplies, and in general household management; but will not be expected to perform more labor than is actually necessary for the desired instruction.

In cookery practical instructions will be given in the means employed in BOILING, BROILING, BAKING, FRYING, and MIXING, as follows:—

BOILING. — Practical illustrations of boiling and steaming, and treatment of vegetables, meats, fish, and cereals, soup-making, etc.

BROILING. — Lessons and practice in: meat, chicken, fish, oysters, etc.

BREAD-MAKING. — Chemical and mechanical action of materials used. Manipulations in bread-making in its various departments. Yeasts and their substitutes.

BAKING. — Heat in its action on different materials in the process of baking. Practical experiments in baking bread, pastry, puddings, cake, meats, fish, etc.

FRYING. — Chemical and mechanical principles involved and illustrated in the frying of vegetables, meats, fish, oysters, etc.

MIXING. — The art of making combinations, as in soups, salads, puddings, pies, cakes, sauces, dressings, flavorings, condiments, etc.

MARKETING AND ECONOMY, ETC. — The selection, and purchase of household supplies. General instructions in systematizing and economizing household work and expenses. The anatomy of animals used as food, and how to choose and use the several parts. Lessons on the qualities of water and steam ; the construction of stoves and ranges ; the properties of different fuels.

THE TEXTILE FABRIC WORK will cover instructions in garment cutting and making; the economical and tasteful use of materials ; millinery, etc.

THE DOMESTIC ECONOMY DEPARTMENT.

Opposite to the drawing-rooms on the fourth floor, and occupying the whole of the west half of the building, are the cooking-class and the textile fabric rooms, lighted in the same manner as the drawing-rooms, warmed by steam, and perfectly ventilated.

THE COOKING-ROOM.

This is 40 x 27 feet, with one large Garland Range, and two gas cooking-stoves, five double tables 5 ft. long by 5 ft. wide, each table to accommodate four pupils, each with her own table space for work, and a small gas-stove on the table between each two, — the accommodations being for classes of twenty. Each table space has a drawer and cupboard below it for all essential utensils, and each pupil must personally go through every process taught. At the other end of the room are pantry closets for teachers' use, and a commodious wash-room with all conveniences for girls, including individual closets for each to keep aprons, clothes, etc.

THE TEXTILE FABRIC ROOM.

This is also 40 x 27 feet, in the north part of the building. The furniture and appliances for teaching domestic handiwork in the cutting and making of garments, upholstery, house-furnishing, hand and machine sewing, etc., and teachers for the same will be provided for the school-year beginning September 5, 1887.

In arranging the laboratory work for boys, the methods of the St. Louis Manual Training School under Dr. C. M. Woodward have been closely followed, while the Department of Domestic Economy has been mainly indebted to

Mrs. Emma P. Ewing, Dean of the School of Domestic Economy, of Iowa State College at Ames, Iowa.

From the Report of the Directors of the Toledo Manual Training School to the Mayor and Common Council of the City.

Since the last report the Department of Domestic Economy has received the earnest attention of your Directors.

It became apparent that not only abstract justice but an enlightened public sentiment demanded that the opportunities for industrial instruction for girls should be as ample and complete as that contemplated for boys.

While the work of this department was not wholly without precedent, yet your Directors deemed it wise to call to their aid an advisory council of ladies to assist in maturing the general plan and details of such instruction; and the advice and direction of such council has been of value in the organization of this department.

Two large and well-lighted rooms on the upper floor of the new building have been set apart for this work, one of which has been furnished with all needed appliances for practical instruction in cookery.

A skilful teacher, Miss N. E. Rawson, a pupil of Mrs. Ewing of the Iowa State College, has been secured, and instruction in cookery is now furnished to large and enthusiastic classes.

The Department of Domestic Economy has been received with great favor and support, and promises to meet the full expectations of those who most warmly encouraged its establishment. The instruction in cookery has proved of great practical value. Next school-year instruction will be furnished in cutting and garment making.

III.

LAWS OF NEW YORK.

[CHAPTER 483.]

An Act to tax gifts, legacies, and collateral inheritances in certain cases. (Passed June 10, 1885; three fifths being present.)

The People of the State of New York, represented in Senate and Assembly, do enact as follows: —

SECT. 1. After the passage of this act, all property which shall pass by will or by the intestate laws of this State from any person who may die seized or possessed of the same while being a resident of the State, or which property shall be within this State, or any part of such property, or any interest therein, or income therefrom, transferred by deed, grant, sale, or gift made or intended to take effect in possession or enjoyment after the death of the grantor or bargainor, to any person or persons, or to a body politic or corporate, in trust or otherwise, or by reason whereof any person, or body politic or corporate shall become beneficially entitled, in possession or expectancy, to any property, or to the income thereof, other than to or for the use of father, mother, husband, wife, children, brother and sister, and lineal descendants born in lawful wedlock, and the wife or widow of a son and the husband of a daughter, and the societies, corporations, and institutions now exempted by law from taxation, shall be and is subject to a tax of five dollars on every hundred dollars of the clear market value of such property and at and after the same rate for any less amount, to be paid to the treasurer of the proper county, and in the city and county of New York to the comptroller thereof, for the use of the State, and all administrators, executors and trustees shall be liable for any and all such taxes until the same shall have been paid, as hereinafter directed; provided that an estate which may be valued at a less sum than five hundred dollars shall not be subject to said duty or tax.

SECT. 2. When any person shall bequeath or devise any property, or interest therein, or income therefrom, to a father, mother, husband, wife, children, brother, and sister, the widow of a son, or a lineal descendant, during life or for a term of years, and the remainder to a collateral heir of the decedent, or to a stranger in blood, or to a body politic or corporate at their decease, or on the expiration of such term, the property so passing shall be appraised immediately after the death of the decedent, at what was the fair market value thereof at the time of the death of the decedent, in the manner hereinafter provided, and after deducting therefrom the value of said life estate, or term of years, the tax prescribed by this act on the remainder shall be immediately due and payable to the treasurer of the proper county, and in the city and county of New York to the comptroller thereof, and, together with the interest thereon, shall be and remain a lien on said property until the same is paid; provided that the person or persons, or body politic or corporate beneficially interested in the property chargeable with said tax may elect not to pay the same until they shall come into the actual possession or enjoyment of such property, or, and in that case, such person or persons, or body politic or corporate, shall give a bond to the people of the State of New York in a penalty three times the amount of the tax arising upon personal estate, with such sureties as the said surrogate may approve, conditioned for the payment of said tax and interest thereon, at such time or period as they or their representatives may come into the actual possession or enjoyment of such property, which bond shall be filed in the office of the surrogate of the proper county; provided, further, that such person shall make a full verified return of such property to said surrogate, and file the same in his office within one year from the death of the decedent and within that period enter into such security and renew the same every five years.

SECT. 3. Whenever a decedent appoints or names one or more executors or trustees and makes a bequest or devise of property to them in lieu of their commissions or allowances which otherwise would be liable to said tax, or appoints them his residuary legatees, and said bequest, devises, or residuary legacies exceed what would be a reasonable compensation for their services, such excess shall be liable to said tax, and the surrogate's court having jurisdiction in the case shall fix such compensation.

SECT. 4. All taxes imposed by this act, unless otherwise herein provided for, shall be due and payable at the death of the decedent, and if the same are paid within one year, interest at the rate of six per cent per annum shall be charged and collected thereon, but if not so paid, interest at the rate of ten per cent per annum shall be charged and collected from the time said tax accrued; provided, that if said tax is paid within six months from the accruing thereof, interest shall not be charged or collected thereon, but a discount of five per cent shall be allowed and deducted from said tax, and in all cases where the executors, administrators, or trustees do not pay such tax within one year from the death of the decedent, they shall be required to give a bond in the form and to the effect prescribed in section two of this act for the payment of said tax, together with interest.

SECT. 5. The penalty of ten per cent per annum imposed by section four hereof for the nonpayment of said tax, shall not be charged where in cases by reason of claims made upon the estate, necessary litigation or other unavoidable cause of delay, the estate of any decedent, or a part thereof, cannot be settled at the end of a year from the death of the decedent, and in such cases only six per cent per annum shall be charged upon the said tax from the expiration of such year until the cause of such delay is removed.

Sect. 6. Any administrator, executor, or trustee having in charge or trust any legacy or property for distribution subject to the said tax shall deduct the tax therefrom, or if the legacy or property be not money, he shall collect the tax thereon, upon the appraised value thereof, from the legatee or person entitled to such property, and he shall not deliver or be compelled to deliver any specific legacy or property subject to tax to any person, until he shall have collected the tax thereon; and whenever any such legacy shall be charged upon or payable out of real estate, the heir or devisee, before paying the same, shall deduct said tax therefrom, and pay the same to the executor, administrator, or trustee, and the same shall remain a charge on such real estate until paid, and the payment thereof shall be enforced by the executor, administrator, or trustee in the same manner that the payment of such legacy might be enforced; if, however, such legacy be given in money to any person for a limited period, he shall retain the tax upon the whole amount, but if it be not in money, he shall make application to the court having jurisdiction of his accounts, to make an apportionment, if the case require it, of the sum to be paid into his hands by such legatees, and for such further order relative thereto as the case may require.

SECT. 7. All executors, administrators, and trustees shall have full power to sell so much of the property of the decedent as will enable them to pay said tax, in the same manner as they may be enabled by law to do for the payment of debts of their testators and intestates, and the amount of said tax shall be paid as hereinafter directed.

SECT. 8. Every sum of money retained by any executor, administrator, or trustee, or paid into his hands for any tax on any property, shall be paid by him, within thirty days thereafter, to the treasurer of the proper county, or in the city and county of New York, to the comptroller thereof, and the said treasurer or comptroller shall give, and every executor, administrator, or trustee shall take, duplicate receipts from him of such payment, one of which receipts he shall immediately send to the comptroller of the State, whose duty it shall be to charge the treasurer or comptroller so receiving the tax with the amount thereof, and shall seal said receipt with the seal of his office, and countersign the same and return it to the executor, administrator, or trustee, whereupon it shall be a proper voucher in the settlement of his accounts; but an executor, administrator, or trustee shall not be entitled to credit in his accounts nor be discharged from liability for such tax unless he shall produce a receipt so sealed and countersigned by the comptroller, or a copy thereof certified by him.

SECT. 9. Whenever any of the real estate of which any decedent may die seized shall pass to any body politic or corporate, or to any person or persons other than the father, mother, husband, wife, lawful issue, wife or widow of a son, or husband of a daughter, or in trust for them, or some of them, it shall be the duty of the executors, administrators, or trustees of such decedent to give information thereof in writing to the treasurer or comptroller of the county where such real estate is situate, within six months after they undertake the execution of their respective duties, or, if the fact be not known to them within that period, then within one month after the same shall have come to their knowledge.

SECT. 10. Whenever any debts shall be proven against the estate of a decedent, after the payment of legacies or distribution of property, from which the said tax has been deducted, or upon which it has been paid, and a refund is made by the legatee, devisee, heir or next of kin, a proportion of the tax so paid shall be repaid to him by the executor, administrator, or trustee, if the said tax has not been paid to the county treasurer, comptroller, or to the State treasurer, or by them if it has been so paid.

SECT. 11. Whenever any foreign executor or administrator shall assign or transfer any stocks or loans in this State, standing in the name of a decedent, or in trust for a decedent, which shall be liable to the said tax, such tax shall be paid to the treasurer or comptroller of the proper county on the transfer thereof, otherwise the corporation permitting such transfer shall become liable to pay such tax, provided that such corporation has knowledge before such transfer that said stocks or loans are liable to said tax.

SECT. 12. When any amount of said tax shall have been paid erroneously to the State treasurer, it shall be lawful for him, on satisfactory proof rendered to the comptroller by said county treasurer or comptroller of such erroneous payment, to refund and pay to the executor, administrator, person, or persons who have paid any such tax in error, the amount of such tax so paid, provided that all such applications for the repayment of such tax shall be made within two years from the date of such payment.

SECT. 13. In order to fix the value of property of persons whose estates shall be subject to the payment of said tax, the surrogate, on the application of any interested party, or upon his own motion shall appoint some competent person as appraiser as often as, and whenever occasion may require, whose duty it shall be forthwith to give such notice by mail, and to such persons as the surrogate may by order direct, of the time and place he will appraise such property; and at such time and place to appraise the same at its fair market value, and make a report thereof in writing to said surrogate, together with such other facts in relation thereto as said surrogate may by order require to be filed in the office of such surrogate; and from this report the said surrogate shall forthwith assess and fix the then cash value of all estates, annuities, and life estates, or term of years growing out of said estate, and the tax to which the same is liable, and shall immediately give notice thereof by mail to all parties known to be interested therein. Any person or persons dissatisfied with said appraisement or assessment may appeal therefrom to the surrogate of the proper county within sixty days after the making and filing of such assessment, on paying, or giving security approved by the surrogate to pay all costs, together with whatever tax shall be fixed by said court. The said appraiser shall be paid by the county treasurer or comptroller out of any funds he may have in his hands on account of said tax, on the certificate of the surrogate, at the rate of three dollars per day for every day actually and necessarily employed in said appraisement, together with his actual and necessary travelling expenses.

SECT. 14. Any appraiser appointed by virtue of this act who shall take any fee or reward from any executor, administrator, trustee, legatee, next of kin or heir of any decedent, or from any other person liable to pay said tax or any portion thereof, shall be guilty of a misdemeanor, and upon conviction in any court having jurisdiction of misdemeanors he shall be fined not less than two hundred and fifty dollars nor more than five hundred dollars, and imprisoned not exceeding ninety days; and in addition thereto the surrogate shall dismiss him from such service.

SECT. 15. The surrogate's court in the county in which the real property is situate of a decedent who was not a resident of the State, or in the county of which the decedent was a resident at the time of his death, shall have jurisdiction to hear and determine all questions in relation to the tax arising under the provisions of this act, and the surrogate first acquiring jurisdiction hereunder shall retain the same to the exclusion of every other.

SECT. 16. If it shall appear to the surrogate's court that any tax accruing under this act has not been paid according to law, it shall issue a citation citing the persons interested in the property liable to the tax to appear before the court on a day certain, not more than three months after the date of such citation, and show cause why said tax should not be paid. The service of such citation, and the time, manner, and proof thereof and fees therefor, and the hearing and determination thereon, and the enforcement of the determination or decree shall conform to the provisions of the Code of Civil Procedure for the service of citations now issuing out of surrogate's courts, and the hearing and determination thereon and its enforcement. And the surrogate or clerk of the surrogate's court shall, upon the request of the district attorney, treasurer of the county, or comptroller of the county of New York, furnish, without fee, one or more transcripts of such decree, as provided in section twenty-five hundred and fifty-three of the Code of Civil Procedure, and the same shall be docketed and filed by the county clerk of any county in the State without fee in the same manner and with the same effect as provided by said section for filing and docketing transcripts of decrees of such courts.

SECT. 17. Whenever the treasurer or comptroller of any county shall have reason to believe that any tax is due and unpaid under this act after the refusal or neglect of the persons interested in the property liable to said tax to pay the same, he shall notify the district attorney of the proper county, in writing, of such failure to pay such tax, and the district attorney so notified, if he have probable cause to believe a tax is due and unpaid, shall prosecute the proceedings in the surrogate's court in the proper county, as provided in section sixteen of this act, for the enforcement and collection of such tax. All costs awarded by such decree that may be collected after the collection and payment of the tax to the treasurer or comptroller of the proper county may be retained by the district attorney hereafter elected or appointed for his own use.

SECT. 18. The surrogate and county clerk of each county shall, every three months, make a statement in writing to the county treasurer or comptroller of his county of the property from which or the party from whom he has reason to believe a tax under this act is due and unpaid.

SECT. 19. Whenever the surrogate of any county shall certify that there was probable cause for issuing a citation and taking the proceedings specified in section sixteen of this act, the State treasurer shall pay or allow to the treasurer or comptroller of any county all expenses incurred for services of citation and his other lawful disbursements that have not otherwise been paid.

SECT. 20. The comptroller of the State shall furnish to each surrogate a book in which he shall enter the returns made by appraisers, the cash value of annuities, life estates, and terms of years and other property fixed by him, and the tax assessed thereon and the amounts of any receipts for payments thereon filed with him, which books shall be kept in the office of the surrogate as a public record.

SECT. 21. The treasurer of each county and the comptroller of the county of New York, shall collect and pay the State treasurer all taxes that may be due and payable under this act, who shall give him a receipt therefor, of which collection and payment he shall make a report under oath to the comptroller on the first Monday in March and September of each year, stating for what estate paid, and in such form and containing such particulars as the comptroller may prescribe; and for all such taxes collected by him and not paid to the State treasurer by the first day of October and April of each year, he shall pay interest at the rate of ten per cent per annum.

SECT. 22. The treasurer of each county and the comptroller of the county of New York hereafter elected or appointed shall be allowed to retain five per cent on all taxes paid and accounted for by him under this act in full for his services in collecting and paying the same, in addition to his salary or fees now allowed by law.

SECT. 23. Any person, or body politic or corporate, shall, upon payment of the sum of fifty cents, be entitled to a receipt from the county treasurer of any county or comptroller of the county of New York, or a copy of the receipt at his option, that may have been given by said treasurer or comptroller, for the payment of any tax under this act, to be sealed with the seal of his office, which receipt shall designate on what real property, if any, of which any decedent may have died seized, said tax has been paid, and by whom paid, and whether or not it is in full of said tax, and said receipt may be recorded in the clerk's office of the county in which said property is situate, in a book to be kept by said clerk for such purpose, which shall be labelled "Collateral Tax."

IV.

LAWYERS are notoriously conservative. Yet so pressing has become the need of doing something to limit "abnormally large fortunes" that the Illinois lawyers are discussing the propriety of limiting by law the amount of money which can be inherited by any one person. At the meeting of the Bar Association of the State of Illinois, in January, 1887, the following among other proceedings were had:—

LIMITING THE AMOUNT OF AN INHERITANCE.

Messrs. Harvey B. Hurd and James A. Connolly, the special committee on the advisability of amending the statutes of descent and wills so as to limit the amount any one person can inherit or take by will from the same decedent, submitted a report, the substance of which is as follows: The Committee in a previous report did not advocate any plan that would carry away an estate from the kin of the decedent, but one that would break it up into smaller portions than is done in the great estates of the present time, and so counteract the growing tendency to mass the wealth of the country in a few hands. The amount a child might take could be limited to $500,000. In the case of an estate of $1,000,000 to which there were as heirs, in the first degree a child, in the second three brothers, and in the third ten other persons, it was recommended that the estate should be divided so as to give $500,000 to the child, $100,000 to each of the three brothers, and $200,000 among the ten persons in the third degree of kinship in equal shares. If more than enough to pay these, the surplus might go to those in the next degree of kinship. No restriction was proposed upon devises for educational or charitable purposes. Upon the question whether such a law would not be evaded by gifts *inter vivos*, and especially in anticipation of approaching death, it was sufficient to say that the law could be so framed as to avoid all gifts that were in their nature testamentary or made with the intent to defeat the law. It was most likely that the law would induce more liberal giving while alive, both to assist dependents and for benevolent purposes.

As to whether the disposition of property upon the death of the owner was within the control of the legislative power of the State, it should be said that there never was a time in the history of the law when such disposition was not regulated by the State. No State, as far as known, had seen fit to impose any constitutional restriction upon the exercise of this power. Both in England

and in this country the power to dispose of property by will was the creature of the statute. The statutes of wills of the different States were almost as variant as the statutes of descent. There was no constitutional restriction upon the right of the legislature to make and change such laws to suit the wishes of the people, nor was there any vested right standing in the way.

There was a most serious and growing discontent over the relations of property to our social and political welfare, but there was a wide difference of opinion as to where the fault lay and how it could be remedied. The committee did not profess to be able to solve the difficulty entirely, but undertook to give some substantial reasons why the recommendations referred to would at least have a favorable tendency, extending with increasing efficiency far into the future. To prevent the accumulation of large estates in particular families, through inheritance and devises, was one of the distinguishing features in the policy of this country and lay at the foundation of our system of government, exercising a salutary influence scarcely less powerful than the elective franchise itself. The committee did not wish to be understood as agreeing with the notion that it was either practicable or desirable to produce an equality as to property, but, on the contrary, indorsed Chancellor Kent's view that "the sense of property is graciously bestowed upon mankind for the purpose of rousing them from sloth and stimulating them to action ; and so long as the right of acquisition is exercised in conformity to the social relations and the moral obligations which spring from them it ought to be sacredly protected." The difficulty was that the laws, as they now stood, fell short in accomplishing what they were designed to do and once did well. The consideration that was uppermost was the safety of property itself.

The committee did not favor in that recommendation such a change in the laws of inheritance as would affect the great majority of estates, but only those that were obnoxious to the spirit of our institutions, the "abnormally large fortunes," which absorbed and took out of circulation large blocks of wealth and gave to their possessors an undue prominence and influence in the affairs of the country. Such accumulations of wealth resulted in discontent that was rapidly and steadily growing. The church could do much by its teachings and ministrations, but it was for the State to correct the source of the unhappy condition of things. Reform could only be accomplished by appealing to the self-interest of the people and not by running counter to it. No man in his natural sympathies would be willing to put his earning in a common pot to be doled out to him from a common crib, or to be driven to his daily toil by a common overseer, — the practical outcome of Socialism. Contentment and safety lay in keeping good the promise of our free institutions, in giving to every man as nearly as might be an equal chance with every other man. Under a wise system of property-law the number of the unsuccessful might be kept down to a small per cent of the whole, — far below the danger point. A more general diffusion of property would not interfere with the carrying forward of great enterprises nor damp the ardor of business if a reasonable limitation were fixed.

Any one can see at a glance that what the Illinois lawyers wish to accomplish can be done much more easily by the succession tax and some of the French rules of inheritance, while at the same time by means of education the people can be made to go up higher.

In the Legislature of Illinois, session of 1887, the following among other proceedings were had:

HOUSE BILL — NO. 233.

35th Assembly Illinois.   January, 1887.

Introduced by Mr. Collins's special committee, January 28, 1887.

First reading January 28, 1887, ordered printed and referred to Committee on Judiciary.

The Special Committee, to whom was referred the preparation of a bill to restrict the amount any person

APPENDIX. 199

or corporation may take by descent or will from the same decedent, respectfully report the following bill.

W. H. COLLINS, Chairman.

A Bill for an Act to restrict the Amount any Person or Corporation may take by Descent or Will from the same Decedent.

SECT. 1. *Be it enacted by the People of the State of Illinois, represented in the General Assembly,* No person shall, by will or testament, devise or bequeath, either in trust or otherwise, more in value or amount, to the same person, than as follows, to wit: To his or her surviving wife or husband, not more than the sum or value of five hundred thousand dollars, or if the estate of decedent, is in whole or in part, in land, not more than fifteen hundred acres of land; to a child of the testator, or of his or her wife or husband, or a legally adopted child, not more than the sum of five hundred thousand dollars, or if the estate or decedent is in whole or in part in land, not more than fifteen hundred acres of land; to the descendants of a child, in case of the death of the child, not more than by this section might be given to the child if she or he were living; to any other person or corporation, not more than the sum or value of one hundred thousand dollars; and any devise or bequest shall be valid to such amount or value, and no more. This section shall not apply to devises or bequests for educational or benevolent purposes.

SECT 2. No person shall be capable of taking by descent or distribution either of the real or personal estate of any person who shall die after the taking effect of this act, more in value and amount as follows, to wit: A surviving husband or wife or child, or a descendant of a child when he can take directly and not by representation, not to exceed five hundred thousand dollars, or if estate of decedent is in whole or in part in land, not more than fifteen hundred acres of land. The descendants of a child taking by representation may take the same that the person he or she represents might have taken if he or she were living. No other person entitled to take by descent or distribution shall be capable of taking from the same decedent more than one hundred thousand dollars. When the estate is more than sufficient to give to the persons first entitled to take the full amount to which they are limited by this act, the balance, or so much thereof as may be sufficient to give to each of them the amount they may take under the limitations contained in this act, shall go to the kin of the deceased standing next in kinship after those first entitled to take under the laws of descent in their degree and their representatives. If there is more than sufficient to give each of those standing in that degree of kinship and entitled to take the amount he or she may take under this act, the balance, or so much thereof as may be sufficient to give to each of those the amount he or she may take under the limitations of this act, shall go to those standing in the next succeeding degree of kinship to the deceased and their representatives. The like rule shall be applied to any surplus, so long as there shall be any, until the whole estate is divided among the kindred of the deceased, preferring those standing nearest to the deceased, to the extent he or she may take under the limitations of this act. When there is not sufficient to give to each of the persons standing in a certain degree of kinship and entitled to share the full amount he or she might take, such part of the estate shall be divided among them and those entitled to take by representation in equal shares, according to the rules of descent heretofore existing. If any balance remains after every person capable of taking the same shall have taken the amount or value he or she is entitled to take, the same shall escheat to the State, as in cases where there is no person capable of inheriting the estate. If in any case a person shall be entitled to take both by descent and by will from the same decedent, the aggregate in value or amount he or she may take shall not exceed the amount he or she is capable of taking by one of these ways.

SECT. 3. The inventory required by law to be made by an executor or administrator, in addition to the matters now required to be stated therein, shall also state the value of each piece or parcel of real estate of which the deceased died possessed of or was in any way entitled, and the total value of the whole estate, real and personal; which statement of the total value of said estate shall be conclusive upon all persons who shall claim any interest in such estate by descent or under the will of the deceased, by virtue of this act, unless the same is changed as hereinafter provided. Upon a sworn petition of one or more persons interested in the estate as heirs or distributors, showing that such total value is too low or too high, the court shall appoint three disinterested persons to revalue the estate, who, being first sworn to make a just and true valuation thereof, shall revalue the same and make return of their valuation, which, unless set aside for fraud or mistake, shall be conclusive as to the rights of all persons claiming or to claim any interest in said estate by descent or under the will of the deceased. In all cases where a specific article or piece of real or personal property is given or devised by will, the value thereof may be inquired into in such way as the Probate Court shall direct.

Sect. 4. In the proof of heirship it shall not be necessary to show other than the heirs who will be entitled to share in the estate, taking into account the limitations contained in this act. Only such heirs or distributees as shall appear to be entitled to share in the estate need be notified of the final settlement by the executor or administrator.

Sect. 5. Before the final settlement of the estate, or with a view to making such final settlement, the court shall find the total value of the estate, and who are the heirs or persons interested therein as heirs, legatees, devisees, or distributees, and the nature and amount of their respective interests, and may order the whole or any part of the real or personal estate, or both, to be sold, and the proceeds brought into court for distribution according to the rights of the parties, or may declare the rights and interests of the respective parties in the respective pieces and parcels of real estate, and may make any and all orders that may be necessary to carry into effect the provisions of this act.

Sect. 6. Every gift, conveyance, transfer, or disposition of any real or personal estate made with intention to defeat the operation of this act shall be void.

Sect. 7. All acts or parts of acts inconsistent with the provisions of this act are hereby repealed.

APPENDIX. 203

Among the acts passed by the Legislature of Illinois, session of 1887, and approved by the governor, is one drawn by Hon. Joshua C. Knickerbocker, judge of the Probate Court of Cook County, the only object of which is to make that court self-sustaining. The act establishes a graduated tax upon estates in providing for a docket fee graduated in proportion to the value of the estate.

FEES OF CLERKS OF PROBATE COURTS.

Approved June 6, 1887. In force July 1, 1887.

. . . . . .

On application for the grant of letters testamentary, of administration, guardianship, or conservatorship, it shall be the duty of the applicant to state in his or her petition the value of all the real and personal estate of such deceased person, infant, idiot, insane person, lunatic, distracted person, drunkard, or spendthrift, as the case may be, and on the grant of letters testamentary, administration, guardianship, or conservatorship, there shall be paid to the clerk of said probate court from the proper estate and charge as costs a docket fee as follows: —

When the estate does not exceed $5,000 . . $5.00
When the estate exceeds $5,000 and does not
    exceed $20,000 . . . . 10.00
When the estate exceeds $20,000 and does
    not exceed $50,000 . . . . 20.00

When the estate exceeds $50,000 and does
   not exceed $100,000 . . . .   50.00
When the estate exceeds $100,000 and does
   not exceed $300,000 . . . . 100.00
When the estate exceeds $300,000 and does
   not exceed $1,000,000 . . . . 250.00
In all cases when such estate amounts to
   $1,000,000 and upwards 1,000.00

In all cases where any deceased person shall leave him or her surviving a widow or children resident of this State, who are entitled out of said estate to a widow's or child's award, and the entire estate, real and personal, of such deceased person shall not exceed $2,000, and in case of any minor whose estate, real and personal, does not exceed the sum of $1,000, and whose father is dead, and in all cases of any idiot, insane person, lunatic, or a distracted person, drunkard, or spendthrift, when such person has a wife or infant child dependent on such person for support, and the entire estate of such person shall not exceed the sum of $2,000, the probate judge (by order of court) shall remit and release to such estate all of the costs herein provided for.

V.

[*From The New York Times, May* 22, 1887.]

COLLEGE ENDOWMENTS.

Not many Americans are really aware of the enormous sums that are annually going to swell the endowments of institutions for learning. A generation ago it is probable that there was not a college in the country of which the available capital was a million dollars. In those days, and in days much later, a gift of thirty thousand dollars or forty thousand dollars to a college was hailed as munificent, and indeed it was so. With the higher rate of interest at that time and with the extremely frugal notions that prevailed among successful merchants of what a professor could live on, such a sum sufficed to give a college a new professorship, of which the incumbent was able to support himself quite as well in a country college as he would have been able to do in a country parish, which was for the most part the alternative. Half a million would have built and "stocked" a college and supplied it with ten professors, even had the income derived from room-rent and tuition been nothing at all.

The first provision for a new college on what we now regard as a liberal scale was that made by Ezra Cornell twenty years ago. A great benefaction it was and remains, but in amount it has since been very greatly outdone. The Johns Hopkins is another example of a college doing valuable work which owes its existence to the generosity of an individual. The endowment of the new university founded by Leland Stanford appears to be considerably over ten millions. It is doubtful whether any university in the world has ever had an endowment at all comparable to this at the beginning. The English universities were slow aggregations from slender beginnings, and it would be misleading to compare them with the university which Senator Stanford proposes to start full-grown. But taking all the colleges of Oxford or of Cambridge together, and allowing for the depreciation in money, or rather confining the comparison to what can be done with the money, it is doubtful whether either university, when the chief colleges had all been founded, say at the end of the seventeenth century, represented an endowment equivalent to that of the new university. This is only the most conspicuous of many gifts for education that in any other age or country would be called princely. A citizen of Worcester, Mass., has lately given a million for the foundation of a university in that city, and has promised to supplement this ample endowment. And perhaps the strongest proof that these great endowments have become so common as to attract no notice is the dismissal, in one line of a dispatch about the will of the late WASHINGTON DE PAUW, of Indiana, of the fact that he has bequeathed $1,250,000 to the De Pauw University.

There is an enormous potentiality of human culture in this recital. It is greatly to be hoped that it may not be defeated by a narrow or temporary interpretation, on the part either of the givers or of their Trustees, of the meaning of the word education. We shall offend nobody, we trust, if we suggest that if a member of the Campbellite Baptist persuasion who had prospered in life were at his death to leave a million dollars for the foundation of a university in which the doctrines of the Campbellite Baptists were to be faithfully taught, and from which all learning and science, falsely so-called, inconsistent with these doctrines should be excluded, educated men and lovers of education would deplore the waste of money involved in such a bequest with such a restriction. Yet this is what is done when any man saddles posterity with his own view of truth and learning. Either his bequest will be useless, or at all events less useful than it might have been, or it will be perverted very far from his own intention, to the moral injury of everybody concerned in the perversion. To found a school of apologetics is quite a different thing from founding a place of education. " I am bound to say," said CARLYLE in his famous address at Edinburgh, "that it does not appear as if endowments were the real soul of the matter. The English, for example, are the richest people in the world for endowments in their universities, and yet it is an evident fact that since the time of BENTLEY you cannot name anybody among them who has gained a European name in scholarship or constituted a point of revolution in the pursuits of men in that way. One man that actually did constitute a revolution was the son of a poor weaver in Saxony, who edited his Tibullus in Dresden in a poor comrade's garret, and who, while editing his Tibullus had to gather peasecods on the streets and boil them for his dinner. That was his endowment. His name was HEYNE." It is safe to suggest that part of the superiority of German scholarship over English comes from the fact that disinterested inquiry has from their origin been the spirit of the German universities, and that the comparative ineffectiveness of the English endowments has come in part from the restrictions imposed by the givers. No man who assumes that what passes for the truth in his own mind or in his own time will pass as such for all time ought to let that notion hamper his gifts for education. He will do the best that is possible by adopting EZRA CORNELL'S excellent motto: "I wish to found a university where any person may obtain instruction in any study."

[*Associated Press Despatch.*]

THE DE PAUW WILL.

Proceedings to set it aside begun by the Dead Millionnaire's First Child.

NEW ALBANY, IND., Aug. 16, 1887.

THIS city is greatly excited to-night over the news of a suit filed here to-day to set aside the will of the late Washington C. De Pauw, who died worth $6,000,000. The attorneys who filed the suit are C. L. and Harry E. Jewett. Their client, the plaintiff, is Mrs. Sarah Ellen McIntosh, wife of J. A. McIntosh, of Salem, Indiana. Mr. De Pauw had three wives. The plaintiff is his first and only child by the first wife. Two sons are living, the only children by the second wife, and the third wife and her daughter survive Mr. De Pauw. To Mrs. McIntosh he willed two poor farms, not worth $5,000 all told, while to his widow and his other three surviving children he willed what will amount to $1,000,000 each. Mrs. McIntosh married against her father's wish, but she thought he forgave her, as he visited her and was otherwise kind to her, and both she and her father were zealous members of the Methodist church. She sues to obtain one-sixth of the estate, and makes the natural heirs and all other legatees defendants.

VI.

[*From the Chicago Tribune, July* 16, 1887.]

THE EDUCATION OF THE FUTURE.

The memorable convention of the National Educational Association stands adjourned. While it has not taken a decided position on the question of manual training, which is destined to be the education of the future, still progress has been made. At the proceedings Thursday the President of the Department of Industrial Education made a strong plea for it and argued that it should go hand in hand with the academical system, and that manual work was favorable in its influence upon the purely intellectual. Professor Woodward of St. Louis, whose manual training school has a national reputation, said: "It has been found that there are methods of teaching and employing children in kindergarten schools, and I believe that boys of fourteen can also be taught in manual training without the book-work suffering a loss." Numerous other instructors gave their testimony as to its value, among them Professor Caruthers of Cincinnati, who said that in that city "drones had become hard-working students." At the dinner given by the Prang Educational Company, which was attended by a large representation of the most prominent people identified with art and industrial education in this country, there were numerous enthusiastic expressions of opinion in favor of the new departure. At the meeting of the Association yesterday morning Gen. Francis Walker, the President of the famous Massachusetts Institute of Technology, whose certificates are of more practical value to a boy entering the world of work than the diploma of any school or college, made an argument for manual training which carried great weight with it, and was listened to with unusual interest.

The report adopted by the convention recognizes the value of the industrial art. The next convention will go farther, we believe, and not only recognize its value, but will act upon it and suggest the plan for adopting it as part of the free-school system. It is growing rapidly. The school exhibit is itself a silent but most powerful argument in its favor and a testimonial to its remarkable growth. It is filled with the results of manual training both in art and industry, and these exhibits dwarf all the others both in interest and in variety. They stand there an unanswerable argument. As the system which educates head and hand together; which arouses enthusiasm in the pupil; which gives an added value to his academical training; which develops the ideal faculty and tends to bring forward the artistic talent of the country; which gives to the boy and girl something which is of practical use to them; which will send them out into the world better prepared to make a living; which gives them habits of industry, and which educates the hand and head to labor instead of educating the wits to avoid labor, — this system is bound to be the future reliance of our free schools. It has come to stay. As President Ordway said in his address: "We need no longer discuss whether the work shall be introduced into the public schools. It is already there and will stay there. What we need to discuss is the methods of teaching and what shall be taught." The Association has recognized the value of the principle. Another Association, we believe, will fix its definite status in the school system, and provide the methods of its operation. It is the education of the future.

THE CHICAGO MANUAL TRAINING SCHOOL CATALOGUE, 1886-87.

Course of Study and Practice.

JUNIOR YEAR.

(1.) *Mathematics.* — Algebra; Geometry.
(2.) *Science.* — Physiology; Physical Geography.
(3.) *Language.* — English Language and Literature; or Latin.

(4.) *Drawing.* — Freehand Model and Object; Projection; Machine; Perspective.

(5.) *Shop-work.* — Carpentry, Joinery, Wood-Turning, Pattern-Making, Proper Care and Use of Tools.

MIDDLE YEAR.

(1.) *Mathematics.* — Geometry; Plane Trigonometry.

(2.) *Science.* — Physics.

(3.) *Language.* — General History; English Literature; or Latin.

(4.) *Drawing.* — Orthographic Projection and Shadows; Line and Brush Shading; Isometric Projection and Shadows; Details of Machinery; Machines from Measurement.

(5.) *Shop-work.* — Moulding, Casting; Forging, Welding, Tempering; Soldering, Brazing.

SENIOR YEAR.

(1.) *Mathematics.* — Mechanics; Book-keeping.

(2.) *Science.* — Chemistry; or Descriptive Geometry and Higher Algebra.

(3.) *Language, etc.* — English Literature, Civil Government, Political Economy; or Latin: or French.

(4) *Drawing.* — Machine from Measurement; Building from Measurement; Architectural Perspective.

(5.) *Machine Shop-work.* — Chipping, Filing, Fitting, Turning, Drilling, Planing, etc. Study of Machinery, including the Management and Care of Steam Engines and Boilers.

Instruction is given each year in the production, properties, and uses of the materials — wood, iron, brass, etc. — used in that year.

Throughout the course, one hour each day is given to Drawing, and two hours each day to Shop-work. The remainder of each school-day is devoted to study and recitation. A diploma testifying to scholarship and skill is given on graduation.

Equipment.

The equipment of the mechanical department of the school is mainly as follows : —

WOOD-ROOMS.

50 Cabinet-maker's-benches; 24 Speed-Lathes; 1 Circular Saw; 1 Scroll Saw; 1 Boring-machine; 1 Planer; 1 Grindstone; 1 Shoot-plane; Bench, Lathe, and General Tools for ninety-six boys.

FOUNDRY.

2 Furnaces; Crucibles, Troughs, Flasks, Trowels, Rammers, Sieves, and other apparatus for sixty-six boys.

FORGE-ROOM.

24 Forges; 23 Anvils; 1 Emery-wheel; 1 Shears; 3 Vises; 1 Blower; 2 Exhaust Fans; Tongs, Hammers, Fullers, Flatters, Swages, etc., for sixty-six boys.

APPENDIX. 215

MACHINE-SHOP.

7 Engine-Lathes, 12-inch swing, 6-feet bed; 1 Engine-Lathe, 16-inch swing, 8-feet bed; 2 Speed-Lathes; 1 Planer, 6-feet bed; 1 Shaper; 1 Drill; 1 Grindstone; 1 Emery-wheel; 15 Benches; 15 Vises; Lathe and Vise Tools, such as Chucks, Boring-bars, Taps, Dies, Hammers, Chisels, Files, etc., sufficient for thirty-three boys; also, 1 Forge, 1 Anvil, 1 Carpenter's-bench, with tools.

Power is supplied by a Corliss engine of 52 horse power and by two steel boilers.

The Work of the School.

The special feature of the school, in which it differs from the ordinary high school, is its MANUAL TRAINING. Notwithstanding the prominence given to this part of its course, experience shows that its mathematical and scientific work need not be inferior to that of the best high schools.

Education, not manufacture, is the idea underlying the manual training. Consequently, the material products of the shops consist chiefly of exercises designed to develop skill in the use of tools. The educational value of construction is also recognized, and the course embraces a number of finished articles.

Some idea of the pupils' work in the drawing and mechanical departments may be obtained from the following partial list of the annual exhibit of June 23, 1886.

JUNIOR CLASS.

In Drawing: Freehand and mechanical drawings of models and tools; problems in Plane Geometry; 4,134 drawings.

In Wood-room: Mortises, tenons, dovetails, panels, picture-frames, foundry-flasks; umbrella-stands; cases of drawers; tables; cylinder office desk; roof-trusses; test-tube racks; 12 cabinet-maker's-benches; gavels; vases; patterns of bells, bell-stands, oilers, hexagonal nuts, globe-valves, pipe-elbows, returns; offsets; core-boxes for the four last named, etc.

MIDDLE CLASS.

In Drawing: Orthographic projection, and line shading, orthographic shadows, machines from measurement; 1,700 drawings.

In Foundry: Moulding and casting of nuts, glands, valves, sheave-pulleys, spur and bevel gears, bells, oil-cups, drawer-pulls, letter-clips, brackets, etc.

In Forge-room: Exercises in drawing, upsetting, bending; open eyes, gate-hooks, hasps, staples, nails, bolts; square-headed lag-screw blanks; hexagon-headed bolt blanks; blacksmith's-tongs; rings; chains; centre-punches, etc., all of iron. In steel, centre-punches; chisels; screw-drivers; diamond-pointed and side lathe-tools; riveting, claw, and ball-pene hammers; brass-turning tools; springs; fullers; drills, etc.

In Wood-room: One complete set of patterns for a 6×9 steam-engine, designed by Assistant-Engineer Bennett.

SENIOR CLASS.

In Drawing: Shaded drawings of globe, safety, and hose valves; details of steam-engine; engine-lathe; drill-press; planer; shaper; stationary and locomotive engines; floor-plans, overhead work, elevations and perspectives of school-building, etc., — all from measurement; 120 drawings.

In Machine-Shop: Exercises in chipping and filing; boring-bar; boring-carriage; clamps and posts for planer; three six-horse-power slide-valve steam-engines made from the castings, to drawings made by the pupils from a finished engine of the same pattern; bolts and nuts for engines; emery-grinder; belt-tightener; taps and dies; milling-arbor; milling-cutters; face-plates, etc.

Among the "projects" of the Senior Class, made from their own drawings, and generally from their own designs, were the following: Four steam-engines (in addition to the three named above); four dynamos; one die-stock, with six taps and six dies; one 40-lb. brass yacht-cannon and carriage; one set geologist's-hammers and chisels; one induction-coil; one link-motion; one speed-lathe. Two of these steam-engines, one 3×6, the other 4×6, were from the pupils' own designs, drawings, and patterns.

Graduates, 1886.

Moritz William Boehm, with Crane Brothers Elevator Company, Teacher of Drawing, Evening High School.

Stuart Dunlevy Boynton.

Gary Nathan Calkins, Massachusetts Institute of Technology.

Allan Montgomery Clement, with Clement, Bane, & Company, Manufacturers.

Charles Locke Etheridge, Sibley College, Cornell University.

William Henry Fahrney, Chicago College of Pharmacy.

Samuel Douglas Flood, Massachusetts Institute of Technology.

Arthur Dewey Hall, with St. Nicholas Toy Manufacturing Company.

Philip Harvey.

Charles Williams Hawkes, with Crane Brothers Elevator Company.

Charles Gilbert Hawley, Sibley College, Cornell University.

John Porter Heywood, Massachusetts Institute of Technology.

Harley Seymour Hibbard, with W. L. B. Jenney, Architect.

Samuel Edward Hitt, Sibley College, Cornell University.

Elbridge Byron Keith, Beloit College.

Henry William Klare, Reedy Elevator Works.

Robert Allan Lackey, with William Sooy Smith & Company, Civil Engineers.

Joseph Dixon Lewis, with N. K. Fairbank & Company, Manufacturers.

James Stuart McDonald, Jr., Assistant Superintendent McDonald-Lawson Manufacturing Company.

Charles Messer.

William Otis Moody.

Ovington Ross, with George P. Ross, Manufacturer.

Albert Scheible, School of Mechanical Engineering, Purdue University.

Herman Schifflin, with Fraser & Chalmers, Manufacturers.

Emil Henry Seemann, with Frederick Seemann, Manufacturer.

Henry Heileman Wait, Hyde Park High School.

Oliver Johnson Westcott, with A. Gottlieb & Company, Civil Engineers.

THE ST. LOUIS MANUAL TRAINING SCHOOL CATALOGUE, 1886-87.

Conditions of Admission.

Candidates for admission to the First-Year class must be at least fourteen years of age, and each must present a certificate of good moral character signed by a former teacher.

They must also pass a good examination on the following subjects: —

1. Arithmetic, including the fundamental rules; common and decimal fractions; the tables of weights, measures, and their use; percentage; and analysis of

miscellaneous problems. Candidates will be examined orally in mental arithmetic, including fractions, mixed numbers, and the higher multiplication-table.

2. Common School Geography, including map-drawing from memory.

3. Spelling and Penmanship.

4. The writing of good descriptive and narrative English, with the correct use of capitals and punctuation.

Candidates for the Second-Year class must be at least fifteen years of age. All that is specified above will be required of them, and, in addition, the book studies of the First-Year class.

Similar requirements apply to those desiring to enter the Third-Year class.

But one new class per year is admitted, namely, in September.

Vacancies may be filled *at any time*, provided the applicants are prepared to enter existing classes.

The Course of Instruction

covers three years, and embraces five parallel lines, — three purely intellectual, and two both intellectual and manual, — as follows : —

First — A course of pure Mathematics, including Arithmetic, Algebra, Geometry, and Plane Trigonometry.

Second — A course in Science and Applied Mathematics, including Physical Geography, Botany, Natural Philosophy, Chemistry, Mensuration, and Book-keeping.

Third—A course in Language and Literature, including English Grammar, Spelling, Composition, Literature, History, and the elements of Political Science and Economy. Latin and French are introduced as electives with English or Science.

Fourth—A course in Penmanship, Free-Hand and Mechanical Drawing.

Fifth—A course of Tool instruction, including Carpentry, Wood-turning, Moulding, Brazing, Soldering, Forging, and Bench and Machine Work in Metals.

The course in Drawing embraces three general divisions:—

1. *Free-Hand Drawing*, designed to educate the sense of form and proportion; to teach the eye to observe accurately, and to train the hand to rapidly delineate the forms either of existing objects or of ideals in the mind.

2. *Mechanical Drawing*, including the use of instruments; geometric constructions; the arrangement of projections, elevations, plans, and sections; also the various methods of representing shades and shadows with pen and brush.

3. *Technical Drawing or Draughting*, illustrating conventional colors and signs, systems of architectural or shop drawings; and at the same time familiarizing the pupil with the proportions and details of various classes of machines and structures.

Students have no option or election as to particular studies, except as regards Latin and French; each must conform to the course as laid down, and take every branch in its order.

The arrangement of studies and shop-work by years is substantially as follows:—

FIRST YEAR.

Arithmetic, completed; *Algebra*, to equations.

English Language, its Structure and use; Study of Selected Pieces; *History* of the United States.

Latin Grammar and Reader may be taken in place of *English*.

Introduction to Science; Physical Geography; Botany.

Drawing, Mechanical and Free-hand; *Penmanship*.

Carpentry and Joinery; Wood-Carving; Wood-Turning.

SECOND YEAR.

Algebra, through Quadratics; *Geometry* begun.

Natural Philosophy; Experimental Work in the Physical Laboratory;[1] *Principles of Mechanics*.

English Composition and Literature; Rhetoric; English History.

Latin [Cæsar] may be taken in place of *English and History*.

Drawing, Line-shading, and Tinting Machines; *Development of Surfaces; Free-Hand Detail Drawing; Isometric Projections*.

Shop-Work — Forging, Drawing, Upsetting, Bending, Punching, Welding, Tempering; Pattern-making, Moulding, Casting, Soldering, and Brazing.

---

[1] In connection with the physical laboratory is a special work-shop containing work-benches, hand tools, two lathes, and a dynamo driven by a small upright steam-engine built by the class of 1886.

THIRD YEAR.

Geometry continued; *Plane Trigonometry; Mensuration.*

English Composition and Literature; History; Ethics, and Political Economy.

French may be taken in place of *English and History*, or in place of the Science study.

Physiology; Elements of Chemistry. Students who have taken Latin, and who intend to enter the Polytechnic School after completing the course in this school, will take History in the place of Physiology and Chemistry.

Book-Keeping.

Drawing, Brush-shading, Machine, and Architectural Drawing.

Work in the Machine-Shop. Bench-work and Fitting, Turning, Drilling, Planing, Screw-cutting, etc. *Study of the Steam-Engine.*

Execution of Project.

The Daily Programme.

The school time of the pupils is about equally divided between mental and manual exercises. The daily session begins at 9 A. M., and closes at 3.30 P. M., thirty minutes being allowed for lunch. Each pupil has daily *three recitations, one hour of drawing or penmanship, and two hours of shop practice.* The order in which these exercises follow each other is shown in the accompanying table.

THE DAILY PROGRAMME—FIRST TERM, 1886-87.

Class.	Div.	9.00 till 11.00.		11.00 till 1.00.		1.00 till 1.30.	1.30 till 3.30.	
Third-Year.	A.	History.	Geometry.	Drawing.	French.	Recess.	Machine-Shop.	French.
	B.	Chemistry.	Drawing.	Machine-Shop.			Geometry.	History.
	C.	Machine-Shop.		Chemistry.	Geometry.		Drawing.	
Second-Year.	A.	Latin.	Physics.	Drawing.	Algebra.	Recess.	Forging-Shop.	Drawing.
	E.	Forging-Shop.	Rhetoric.	Rhetoric.	Physics.		Algebra.	Algebra.
	I.	Physics.	Rhetoric.	Forging-Shop.			Drawing.	Algebra.
	O.	Moulding-Shop.		Physics.	Drawing.		Latin.	
First-Year.	A.	Wood-working Shop.		English.	Arithmetic.	Recess.	Science.	Drawing.
	E.	Science.	Drawing.	Wood-working Shop.			Latin.	Arithmetic.
	I.	Drawing.	English.	Arithmetic.	Science.		Wood-working Shop.	
	O.	Drawing.	Arithmetic.	Wood-working Shop.			Latin.	Science.

REMARKS.—At least once a week in every class the literary work takes the form of reading and studying classic English. In the lower classes, Penmanship takes the place of Drawing occasionally, according to needs.

Diploma and Certificate.

Students who complete the course with credit in all its details will receive the diploma of the school.

Before receiving a diploma of the school, each student must execute, either alone or in connection with certain specified students, a project satisfactory to the managers of the school. The *project* consists in the actual construction of a machine. The finished machine must be accompanied by a full set of the working-drawings according to which the machine is made. If it is not feasible to construct the patterns for castings of such machine, proper directions for their construction must accompany the drawings.

School Building and Accommodations.

THE TWO CARPENTER AND TURNING SHOPS.

Each wood-working shop has uniform accommodations for a class of twenty-four pupils.

Each pupil has one of the uniform sets of hand edge-tools for his exclusive use, kept in a locked drawer. For the care and safety of these tools he is held responsible.

The school has forty-eight speed-lathes for wood-turning, forty-eight benches, vises, and common (non-cutting) tools, and 144 individual sets of edge-tools in as many drawers.

THE MOULDING, BRAZING, AND SOLDERING ROOM.

This shop contains twenty-four benches and sets of tools, flasks, etc., for moulding. A small gas-furnace for melting alloys, and ladles for casting, furnish sufficient practice to test the accuracy of patterns and moulds. Separate benches and furnaces are provided for brazing and soldering.

THE FORGING-SHOP.

The first floor of the building is devoted to metal work, and comprises the machine and blacksmith shops. The blacksmith-shop is forty feet square, and has its complete equipment of twenty-two forges, anvils, tubs, and sets of ordinary hand tools. The blast is supplied by a power blower, and a large exhaust fan[1] keeps the shop reasonably free from smoke and gas.

THE MACHINE-SHOP

is 40 × 50 feet. It possesses an equipment of sixteen engine-lathes, as follows: eight 14-inch Putnam lathes from Fitchburg, Massachusetts; three 14-inch Star lathes from Providence, Rhode Island; and five 15-inch Powell lathes from Worcester, Massachusetts. Also four speed-lathes, a post-drill, a planer 21-inch by 21-inch

---

[1] This fan, a "Sturtevant" with a delivery of 18″ by 23″, was presented to the school by Mr. Sturtevant, the inventor.

by 5 feet, a small hand planer, a 25-inch gooseneck drill, a shaper of 15 inches stroke, 2 grindstones, a double emery-grinder and a gas-forge[1] and anvil. Ten vises and benches afford opportunity for bench-work. The shop is furnished for a class of twenty students at once.

In the summer of 1886 important changes were made in the shop. The large engine was taken out and on the floor space thus gained four additional Putnam lathes were placed. The entire shop was double-floored and otherwise improved.

The present engine-room is below this shop. The engine is capable of about fifty horse-power. It has a 14-inch cylinder and 12-inch stroke, and runs at the rate of 170 revolutions per minute. It was built specially for the school by Messrs. Smith, Beggs, & Rankin, of St. Louis. The steam-generating apparatus of the University consists of a battery of three large steel boilers, set and furnished in the most approved manner. These boilers furnish heat for the entire group of University buildings, as well as steam for the engine in the shop. The equipment of steam power furnishes to pupils of the Third-Year class the means of becoming familiar with machinery on a practical scale.

[1] The gas-forge is furnished with an air jet by the Westinghouse brake, which was presented to the school by the Westinghouse Brake Company. The air-pump of this machine is also used to exhaust the receiver in the physical laboratory.

Details of Shop Instruction.

The shop instruction is given similarly to laboratory lectures. The instructor at the bench, machine, or anvil, fully explains the principles to be used or illustrated, executes in the presence of the whole class the day's lesson, giving all needed information, at times using the blackboard. When it is possible the pupils make working-drawings of the piece or model to be executed, and questions are asked and answered, that all obscurities may be removed. The class then proceeds to the execution of the task, leaving the instructor to give additional help to such as need it. At a specified time the lesson ceases and the work is brought in, commented on, and marked. It is not necessary that all the work assigned should be finished; the essential thing is that it should be well begun and carried on with reasonable speed and accuracy.

All the shop-work is disciplinary ; special trades are not taught, nor are the articles manufactured for sale; as a rule the products of the shop have no value except as exercises, illustrating typical forms and methods.

The object of the school is education, and none of the class exercises, whether in the shop, the drawing or the recitation room, can be supposed to have any pecuniary value. The most instructive tasks have no outcome except in the intelligence and skill of the student himself.

The scope of a single trade is too narrow for educational purposes. Manual education should be as broad and liberal as intellectual. A shop which manufactures for the market, and expects a revenue from the sale of its products, is necessarily confined to salable work; and a systematic and progressive series of lessons is impossible, except at great cost. If the object of the shop is education, a student should be allowed to discontinue any task or process the moment he has learned to do it well. If the shop were intended to make money, the students would be kept at work on what they could do best, at the expense of breadth and versatility. In a factory intellectual life and activity is not aimed at; its sole object is the production of articles for the market. In a manual training school everything is for the benefit of the boy; he is the most important thing in the shop; *he is the only article to be put upon the market.*

Even in manual education the chief object is mental development and culture. Manual dexterity is but the evidence of a certain kind of mental power; and this mental power, coupled with a familiarity with the tools the hand uses, is doubtless the only basis of that sound practical judgment and ready mastery of material forces and problems which always characterizes one well fitted for the duties of active, industrial life.

Hence, the primary object is the acquirement of that mental clearness and intellectual acumen which is the natural outgrowth of logical processes fully comprehended and intelligently executed. This thoughtful activity results in skill in the use of tools and materials. The production of specific articles is a secondary and far inferior consideration. Moreover the training must be *general*, that its possible economic application may have the widest range. We therefore abstract all the mechanical processes and manual arts and typical tools of the trades and occupations of men, arrange a systematic course of instruction in the same, and then incorporate it in our system of education. Thus, without teaching any one trade, we teach the essential mechanical principles of all.

Accordingly, the shop-training is gained by regular and carefully graded lessons designed to cover as much ground as possible, and to teach thoroughly the uses of ordinary tools. This does not imply the attainment of sufficient skill to produce either the fine work or exhibit the rapidity of a skilled mechanic.

How the Use of Tools is Taught.

The tools of a shop are not given out all at once; they are issued as they are needed, and as a rule, to all the members of the class alike.

I. CARPENTRY.

In carpenter work the tools used are: the crosscut, tenon, and rip saws; steel square, try square, bevel and gauge, hammer, mallet, rule, and dividers, oil stones and slips. And among edge tools: the jack and smoothing planes, chisels and gouges. Braces and bits, jointer planes, compass saws, hatchets and other tools are kept in the shop tool-closet to be used as needed.

The saw and the plane with the square, chisel, and gouge are the foundation tools, and to drill the pupils in their use numerous lessons are given, varied only enough to avoid monotony. The pupil being able to plane a piece fairly well, and to keep to the line in sawing, the first and most important step is to learn to "lay out" his piece properly. This requires great care and attention to details, and precision. Self-taught workmen are always lacking here. The next step is to teach the use of the chisel in producing simple joints of various kinds. The particular shapes are given with the intent to familiarize the pupil with the customary styles and methods of construction.

Previous to the execution of a lesson in wood, each pupil is required to make a working-drawing of the same in his book, inserting all necessary dimensions in figures.

The different sizes of the same tool, a chisel for instance, require different care and methods of handling; and the means of overcoming irregularities and defects in material form another chapter in the instruction to be given.

With the introduction of each tool the pupils are taught how to keep the same in order. They are taught that sharp tools are absolutely necessary to good work.

II. WOOD-TURNING.

Five or six tools only are used, and from previous experience the pupils know how to keep them in order. At first a large gouge only is used, and the pupils are taught and drilled in its use in roughing-out and producing cylinders and cones; then concave and double-curve surfaces; then in work comprising all these, — all in wood-turning with the grain. A wide chisel follows, and its use in conjunction with the gouge is taught. After this, a smaller gouge, chisel, and parting-tool, and a round point are given, and a variety of shapes are executed. Next comes turning across the grain; then bored and hollow work, chucking, and the various ways of manipulating wood on face-plates, mandrels, etc. Finally, turning of fancy woods, polishing, jointing, and construction work

III. FORGING.

Work in the blacksmith-shop is in one essential feature different from any other kind. Wood or cold iron will wait any desired length of time while the pupil considers how he shall work, but here comes in temperature subject to continual change. The injunction is imperative to "strike while the iron is hot," and hence quick work is demanded, — a hard thing for new hands. To obviate this difficulty bars of lead are used, with which the lesson is first executed, while all the particulars of form and the methods of holding and striking are studied. The lead acts under the hammer very nearly like hot iron, and permits every operation on the anvil except welding.

The various operations of drawing, bending, upsetting, punching, welding, tempering, etc., are learned in connection with the fabrication of hooks, stirrups, chains, swivels, tongs, hammers, and machine-tools.

The final exercises in the shop consist in the construction of a set of tools which the pupil will himself use in the machine-shop during his third year.

One of the most difficult lessons in the art of the smith is that of managing the fire. The various kinds of heat are explained and illustrated, the habits of economy of both iron and heat are inculcated. The exercises in forging occupy the shop time for thirty weeks.

IV. PATTERN MAKING AND MOULDING.

The course in pattern making and moulding was greatly extended during the past year. These subjects, with some exercises in soldering, now occupy ten weeks (that is, one hundred hours).

In connection with the making of patterns, their use is shown by brief exercises in moulding. Castings are made of lead or type-metal and plaster. Though very little moulding or casting is done by the students, enough practice is given to illustrate the principles and explain the use of technical terms.

Last year a complete set of patterns (that is, a large number of sets of patterns) of a three or four horse-power engine was made, moulded, and cast in plaster. In this way several barrels of plaster were used and hundreds of models, more or less perfect, were produced. In some instances ornamental or art forms were moulded and cast.

V. MACHINE-SHOP WORK.

In the machine shop it is obviously out of the question to furnish a class of twenty pupils with a lathe, planer, drill, etc., *each*. The cost of such tools and the size of such a shop puts the matter beyond discussion.

Hence it is not possible to have all the pupils in a class of twenty performing the same exercise at once, as is the case in the shops just described. Nevertheless, this fact does not interfere with the use of systematic lessons and uniform practice. By exercises suited to the uses of each machine, and to bench-work, and by regular rotation of the class, each pupil does the same work. The verbal instruction and illustration at the machine for any lesson is given to the whole class at once, while a system of printed cards always within the pupil's reach, serves to refresh his memory without taxing the instructor when several days intervene between the instruction to the class and the pupil's performance. Thus it is practicable to secure in a large degree the benefits of the class system.

The course includes work at the —

(*a.*) *Bench:* Use of hammer and chisel, file and scraper, hand dies, taps and reamers.

(*b.*) *Hand-Lathe:* Use of hand tools, drilling, counter-sinking, filing, and polishing.

(*c*) *Engine-Lathe:* Turning, boring with bar and lathe-tool, screw-cutting, external and internal chucking and machine-fitting.

(*d.*) *Drill Press:* Drilling and boring.

(*e.*) *Planer and Shaper:* Producing flat or curved surfaces and fittings.

(*f.*) Care of tool-room, the preparation of shop drawings; study of the engine and boilers.

(*g.*) Construction of a machine.

THE SMALL AMOUNT OF SHOP PRACTICE.

The time spent in shop-work has never exceeded two hours per day, unless the boys have voluntarily remained after hours, that is, after 3.30 o'clock, for additional practice. Moreover, from these two hours should be subtracted fully fifteen minutes for washing, dressing, etc. A week, therefore, represents less than nine hours of actual work in a shop. Hence, in placing a value upon the time spent it should be remembered that a "day's work" is all the boys have per week. For carpentry and wood-turning they have three hundred and eighty hours, or thirty-eight days in all ; in forging, moulding, brazing, and soldering, during the second year, three hundred and eighty-hours ; in iron-fitting, turning, finishing, etc., three hundred and eighty hours. They are thus boys of very limited practice, and while they ought to have intelligent ideas of tools and their uses, of the laws of mechanism, of the properties of wood, iron, steel, and brass, and understand the meaning and force of mechanical words and technical terms, one ought not to expect finished work from their hands.

Literary and Scientific Culture.

It has not been thought necessary to detail the work done on the familiar subjects of mathematics, science, and literature. The simultaneous development and discipline of intellectual and physical faculties is the main object of the course. The aim is to do thorough work ; to lay out a fair course of study and to cover it well. There is no laxity in book-work in consequence of the introduction of manual features in the daily programme.

The General Theory of the School.

The Manual Training School is not an asylum for dull or lazy boys. It clearly recognizes the pre-eminent value of and necessity for intellectual development and discipline. In presenting some novel features in its course of instruction, the managers do not assume that in other schools there is too much intellectual and moral training, but that there is too little manual training for ordinary American boys. This school exacts close and thoughtful study with tools as well as with books. It proposes by lengthening the usual school-day a full hour, and by abridging somewhat the number of daily recitations, to find time for drawing and tool work, and thus to secure a more liberal intellectual and physical development, — a more symmetrical education.

"Manual training is essential to the right and full development of the human mind." Certain intellectual faculties, such as observation and judgment in inductive reasoning, cannot be properly trained except through the instrumentality of the hand. The proverbial caution of the practical manipulator, and his distrust of mere theory (which means reasoning based on assumed, not real facts), shows how unsafe is reasoning not founded on the closest observation and intimate knowledge of the facts of nature. Manual training cultivates the judgment rather than the memory.

Every one seems to admit that it is a good thing for a boy, in addition to his literature, science, and mathematics, to understand the theory and practical use of ordinary tools; to be able to make and read drawings as used in the arts; and to have some cultivation in the graces of form and ornament. The question is, Where shall he get these things? Some say in private shops and offices; some say in private schools; others say at home during vacation. Some assume that it is clear even without experiment that such things are taught more quickly and better at home than at school. Now, as a matter of fact, most boys don't learn these things anywhere. Those who learn the theory and use of tools in private (commercial) shops and offices do so at great expense of what is more valuable than money; the training generally costs an unreasonable waste of time, a sacrifice of the literary and scientific parts of education, often a sacrifice of wholesome associations; and generally one gets only a narrow manual training after all. An experience of many years enables the Director to say that the general use of tools and mechanical processes, together with ordinary draughting (drawing and tool-work should go hand in hand), can be taught more quickly, far better, and at much less cost at a properly equipped school than at home. No one who has seen what is accomplished in this direction in a good school can for a moment be in doubt about the superiority of the school method.

THE HABIT OF THINKING.

" I well know how firmly fixed is the old curriculum of study in the secondary schools, by how many traditions it is supported, and how unfamiliar and strange the manual elements appear to teachers. A visit to our school generally removes prejudice and puts the discipline in a new light. Unfavorable criticism usually is from those who have never seen a manual training school, and as would be expected some of the things said about us are marked by a great lack of appreciation of our methods and results.

" For instance, an Illinois professor said a few years ago that hammering wood was such a different matter from hammering iron that not only was skill in one branch of no value in the other, but that it was a positive hinderance. At once the argument was caught up by the opponents of manual training, and we were entertained by learned discussions of the various arts of hammering, by those who really knew nothing about them. It is as though one should insist that a knowledge of French is a hinderance to the learning of Spanish, or a knowledge of Latin an obstacle to the mastery of Greek. It has been asserted by critics that there can be no such thing as a general training in the use of tools, and they point to the cramped muscles and unintelligent automatonism of a man who for years has headed pins or stamped small pieces of tin, as exhibiting the baneful effects of manual training! Is it possible that such people know what we mean by manual training?

"Can they be aware that, in no American manual training school (and there are no such schools in France, or Germany, or Russia) is the number of hours devoted to the entire series of wood-working tools over four hundred? That the stage of mechanical habit is never reached? *That the only habit actually acquired is that of thinking?* That no blow is struck, no line drawn, no motion regulated, from muscular habit? That the quality of every act springs from the conscious will accompanied by a definite act of judgment? Can such a limited training produce a high degree of manual skill? Of course not. We have distinctly stated that our pupils do not become skilled mechanics, nor do we teach them the full details of a single trade. The tools whose theory, care, and use we teach are representative, and the processes which we teach, just far enough to make every step clear and experimentally understood, equally underlie a score of trades. I say experimentally understood, by which I mean that it is not enough to know that a certain outline is to be produced, or a certain adaptation is to be secured, but one must know just the forces to be directed, the motions needed, and in their order, and all as the result of the closest attention and steady intellectual activity.

"What, then, is this so-called manual training but continuous mental discipline? I have already spoken of the mental effect of science study. I claim equally beneficial effects for the thoughtful study of the theory and use of typical tools."

THE DEVELOPMENT OF NATURAL APTITUDES.

It occasionally happens that students who have special aptitudes in certain directions find great difficulty in mastering subjects in other directions. In such cases it is often the best course to yield to natural tastes, and to assist the student in finding his proper sphere of work and study. A decided aptitude for handicraft is sometimes coupled with a strong aversion to and unfitness for abstract and theoretical investigations. There can be no doubt that, in such cases, more time should be spent in the shop, and less in the lecture and recitation room. On the other hand, great facility in the acquisition and use of language is often accompanied by a great lack of either mechanical interest or power. When such a basis is discovered, the lad should unquestionably be sent to his grammar and dictionary, rather than to the laboratory or draughting-room. It is confidently believed that the developments of this school will prevent those serious errors in the choice of a vocation which often prove so fatal to the fondest hopes.

DIGNITY OF INTELLIGENCE IN LABOR.

One great object of the school is to foster a higher appreciation of the value and dignity of intelligent labor, and the worth and respectability of laboring-men. A boy who sees nothing in manual labor but mere brute force, despises both the labor and the laborer. With the acquisition of skill in himself, comes the ability and willingness to recognize skill in his fellows. When once he appreciates skill in handicraft, he regards the skilful workman with sympathy and respect.

Again, it is highly desirable that a larger proportion of intelligent and well-educated youth should devote their energies to manual pursuits or to the development of mechanical industries, both for their own sakes and for the sake of the occupations and for society.

Undoubtedly the common belief is that it requires no great amount of brains or intelligence to be a mechanic; and those who go through ordinary higher schools are not expected by their teachers to be mechanics. Every bright farmer's boy, every gifted son of a mechanic, if he but stay in school, is sure to be stolen away from the occupation of his father and led into the ranks of the "learned professions."

This loss of the best minds, and the lack of the results of a generous education does much to give color to popular prejudice, and to keep down mechanic arts in the estimation of all. This result is most unfortunate for society. It creates distinctions which ought not to exist, and gives rise to false estimates of the comparative value of the various kinds of intellectual culture. "The successful conduct of any business demands and develops a special scholarship, which is not less valuable as a means of discipline because it is so useful as a source of wealth. The business man may be narrow, but so may the scholar; and in either case, the narrowness results not so much from the necessities of the vocation as from the character of the man."[1]

Hitherto, men who have cultivated their minds have neglected their hands; and those who have labored with their hands have found no opportunity to cultivate their brains. The crying demand to-day is for intellectual combined with natural training. It is this want that this school aims to supply. Its motto is, "The cultured mind, the skilful hand."

THE GENERAL VALUE OF MANUAL TRAINING.

It is not assumed that every boy who enters this school is to be a mechanic. Some will find that they have no taste for manual arts, and will

[1] Prof. S. Waterhouse.

turn into other paths, — law, medicine, or literature. Some who develop both natural skill and strong intellectual powers will push on through the Polytechnic School into the realms of professional life as engineers and scientists. Others will find their greatest usefulness as well as highest happiness in some branch of mechanical work, into which they will readily step when they leave school. All will gain intellectually and morally by their experience in contact with *things*. The grand result will be an increasing interest in manufacturing pursuits, more intelligent mechanics, more successful manufacturers, better lawyers, more skilful physicians, and more useful citizens.

THE RESULTS OF EXPERIENCE.

The school is now in its seventh year. From the start it has been well patronized, and vacant seats have been few. The enrolment shows a steady increase.

The zeal and enthusiasm of the students have been developed to a most gratifying extent, extending into all the departments of work. The variety afforded by the daily programme has had the moral and intellectual effect expected, and an unusual degree of sober earnestness has been shown. The wholesome moral effect of a course of training which interests and stimulates the ardor of the student is most marked. Parents observe the beneficial influence of *occupation*. The suggestions of the day fill the mind with healthy thoughts and appetites during the leisure hours. Success in drawing or shop-work has often had the effect of arousing the ambition in mathematics and history, and *vice versa*. Gradually the students acquire two most valuable habits which are certain to influence their whole lives; namely, precision and method.

The habit of working from drawings and to nice measurements has given the students a confidence in themselves altogether new. This is shown in the readiness with which they undertake the execution of small commissions in behalf of the school, and the handiness which they display at home. From the testimony of parents, the physical, intellectual, and moral effect of the school is exceedingly satisfactory.

THE RECORD OF THE GRADUATES.

Four classes have graduated from the school. Much interest has been expressed in their records as affording some clew to the influence of their training in the school. It has therefore been thought best to give a full list of the names and present occupations of the first three classes as fully as known. At the same time it should be borne in mind that the full influence of the school is to be found only by following the careers of all who have been for a longer or a shorter time under its influence. Only about one half of those who attend the school remain to graduate, and the influence of the training has been scarcely less marked upon those who have been in the school two years than upon the graduates. Moreover, all the graduates are still too young to afford material for very definite conclusions.

These first two classes had no opportunity while in school to study Latin; consequently when they have sought to enter Polytechnic schools or colleges requiring Latin before admission they have been somewhat embarrassed to obtain the necessary instruction in Latin. All the present classes have had opportunity to study Latin in the school.

Class of 1883.

Henry H. Bauer, Farmer, Dorchester, Ill.

John Boyle, Jr., B. E., Fifth-year student in Mining Engineering, Washington University.

John L. Bryan, Journeyman in Pipe Works, Washington, Mo.

Alexander W. Buchanan, Student in Mechanical Engineering, Cornell University.

Peyton T. Carr, Clerk office of Insurance Commissioner.

Edward E. Davidson, Partner in Real Estate business, St. Paul, Minn.

Cornelius V. De Jong, Machinist.

Harry Deitrich, Machinist, Draughtsman, Patternmaker, etc., Brass Foundry, St. Louis.

William S. Dodd, Collector Laclede Gas Works, St. Louis.

Henry F. Dose, Student University of Illinois.

Wm. J. Downton, Architect's office.

Theo. Gluck, Junior Class in Mining Engineering, Washington University.

S. D. Hayden, Clerk in Southeastern Railway Office.

Robert L. Hyatt, Farmer, St. Louis County.

Conrad S. Ittner, Jr., Bricklayer.

Wm. B. Ittner, Student in Architecture, Cornell University.

Albert L. Johnson, Senior Class Civil Engineering, Washington University.

Wm. Love, Assistant Engineer Missouri Pacific Railway.

Harry W. Lytance.

Robert H. McMath, B. E., with Adolphus Meier & Co., St. Louis.

Otto L. Mersman, Merchant, St. Louis.

Wm. G. Nixon, Clerk Supply Department, Iron Mountain Railway.

Everett G. Phillips, Engineer and Shoemaker, St. Louis.

Wm. K. Roth, Grocer, St. Louis.

Justus W. Schmidt, Draughtsman Architect's office.

Greenfield Sluder, Medical Student.

Jules C. Smith, Machinist.

Herbert Taylor, Draughtsman.

John P. Thul, Senior Class, Dynamic Engineering, Washington University.

John F. Vallé, Clerk in Commission House.

Class of 1884.

Grant Beebe, Junior Class, Dynamic Engineering, Washington University.

A. Theodore Bruegel, Junior Class, Mechanical Engineering, Lehigh University.

Geo. R. Carothers, Principal Technical School, Cincinnati, Ohio.

Walter R. Coles, Clerk with John Coles & Co.

Claude N. Comstock, Junior Class in Civil Engineering, Columbia College, N. Y.

Geo. D. Eaton, Principal High School, Marine, Ill.

Alfred C. Einstein, Stenographer St. L. & S. F. Ry.

Hamilton R. Gamble, Clerk wholesale drug store.

Charles D. Grayson, Practical Mailer, St. Louis.

Geo. N Hinchman, Jr., Draughtsman in Office of Patent-lawyer.

Ernest C. Klipstein, Draughtsman.

Charles A. Langdon, Clerk.

James L. Marks, Machinist, Shops Mo. Pac. Ry. St. Louis.

Constant Mathey, Salesman with Mermod, Jaccard, & Co.

Alex. D. Mermod, Ranchman, Poncha Park, Col.

Ralph H. Miller, Principal Toledo Manual Training School, Toledo, Ohio.

George S. Mills, Teacher of Drawing, Toledo Manual Training School.

William O'Keefe, Shipping Clerk of Machinery.

Otto H. Olfe, Draughtsman and Superintendent with W. E. Bent, Architect, St. Louis.

Harry M. Pflager, Head Draughtsman Pullman Car Works, St. Louis.

John H. Pope, Junior Class in Civil Engineering, Washington University.

Edward L. Pretorious, Clerk business department Westliche Post, St. Louis.

Wm. F. Richards, Clerk in office of Vandalia R. R.

Harry C. Scott, Clerk in Railroad office.

Percy S. Silver, Manufacturer, Lexington, Mo.

Charles F. Springer, Chicago.

H. Reed Stanford, Junior Class Dynamic Engineering, Washington University.

Homer Wise, Foreman Collier Lead and Oil Works, St. Louis.

Edmund H. Wuerpel, Student of Drawing and Architecture.

Harry B. Wyeth, Sophomore Class, Michigan University, will study law.

Class of 1885.

Wm. F. Barnes, Teacher Manual Training School, Eau Claire, Wis.

Hatcher Bates, Farmer, Mo.

A. M. Bumann, Teacher Manual Training, Omaha High School, Neb.

King Charles Barton, travelling in Europe.

Judson S. Bemis, with Bemis Brothers Bag Co.

Edgar L. Brother, Teacher Manual Training, Swathmore College, Penn.

Thomas W. Booth, St Louis, Law Student.

Albert H. Buck, Draughtsman American Brake Co., St. Louis.

Edward H. Chapman, Farmer.

Frederick A. Chouteau, Teacher Manual Training, Swathmore College, Penn.

Geo. W. Danforth, Cadet U. S. Naval Academy, Annapolis.

H. G. Ellis, Student School of Fine Arts, Washington University

Arthur Feickert, Baker, Belleville, Ill.

Charles O. Fischer, Office of Civil Engineer.

Wm. F. Hopper, Apprentice at Stove and Machine Pattern-making, St. Louis.

Clarence H. Howard, General Foreman Motive Power, Mo. Pac. Ry.

H. F. S. Kleinschmidt, Student Washington University, expects to teach.

Albert Koberle, Student Sophomore Class, Washington University.

Wm. P. Laing, Machinist, St. Louis.

Edward L. Lange, Clerk Hardware Store.

Ernest E. Lazar, Baldridge Type-writing Co.

Louis D. Lawnin, Clerk N. O. Nelson Mfg. Co.

Edward H. Lebens, Student Sophomore Class, Washington University.

John J. Lichter, Jr., Student Sophomore Class, Washington University.

Wm. Alex. Magee, Practical Electrician.

Frank W. Morse, Foreman Wabash Repair Shops, St. Louis.

Frank E. Nulsen, Student Sophomore Class, Washington University.

Geo. R. Olshausen, Student Sophomore Class, Washington University.

Charles M. Parker, Student Sophomore Class, Troy Polytechnic Institute.

Frank E. Reel, at home.
Louis C. Rohlfing, Medical Student.
Edward H. Rattman, Stenographer.
James L. Sloss, Student.
Edward Smith, Lumber Business.
Geo. M. Stedman, Agricultural Works, Aurora, Ind.
J. Harrison Steedman, Student Sophomore Class, Washington University.
Hamilton W. Stone, Teller, —— Bank, St. Louis.
Wm. T. Treadway, Machinist Mo. Pac. Shops, St. Louis.
Harry L. Whitman, in business with his father.
Charles H. Wright, Teacher Manual Training School, Denver University, Col.

In submitting the above report of the condition, methods, aims, and results, of the school during its six and a half years, the Director is gratified by the thought that in spite of its many shortcomings the school has served to demonstrate the entire feasibility of incorporating the elements of intellectual and manual training in such a way that each is the gainer thereby; and that he has correctly read the public demand for an education which shall insure the most valuable mental discipline, at the same time that it gives knowledge and skill of great intrinsic worth.

BOOKS OF ESSAYS AND CRITICISM.

James Vila Blake's Essays.—Cloth, 12mo,
216 pages, $1.00.

The essays of Mr. Blake will surprise and delight a l lovers of good English prose. He has made a contrib u tion of lasting value to our literature, in a form so co n densed and so original as to inevitably attract and hol d the attention of thoughtful readers. . . . . Shar p- ness of vision, too, makes this essayist a helper to t h understanding and the sight of slower mortals. He oft e touches to the quick, and reveals the spring of some o the most puzzling questions by his sure but gen tl insight.—*Chicago Tribune.*

St. Solifer, with Other Worthies and Un= worthies.—By JAMES VILA BLAKE. Cloth, 12mo, 179 pages, $1.00. Paper, 50 cents.

Fourteen short stories and sketches of unusual quality. . . . The papers are the recreation of a finely touched mind; we should suppose that any one who can appreciate their delicate qualities might be warranted in complimenting himself.—*Literary World.*

Legends From Storyland.—By JAMES VILA BLAKE. Cloth, square 16mo, 87 pages, illustrated, 50 cents.

The style in which these legends are written is charm ing and adjusts itself with wonderful felicity to th e nature of the themes. But our pleasure was seriousl y diminished when we found that the author classes th e miracles of the Old and New Testaments with othe r legends. . . . It is sad indeed when powers of such an order are used . . . etc.—*The Living Church.*

Browning's Women.—By MARY E. BURT.
With an introduction by Edward Everett Hale, D. D., LL. D. Cloth, 16mo, 236 pages, $1.00.

We can cordially recommend her little volume to not only individual readers, but to members of the Browning Clubs who are endeavoring to make a special study of the poet.—*Boston Transcript.*

The Legend of Hamlet, Prince of Denmark,
as found in the works of Saxo Grammaticus and other writers of the Twelfth Century. By GEORGE P. HANSEN. Square 18mo, 57 pages, paper, 25 cents; cloth, 50 cents.

Charles H. Kerr & Co., Pubs., 175 Dearborn St., Chicago

BOOKS OF RELIGION AND ETHICS.

The Morals of Christ.—A comparison with the contemporaneous systems of Mosaic, Pharisaic and Græco-Roman ethics. By Austin Bierbower. Paper, 16mo, 200 pages, 50 cents; cloth, $1.00.

Mr. Bierbower's book affords an admirable example of the scientific treatment of an historical subject. He has carefully analyzed the old-world ethical systems which chiefly concern the modern civilized world, and in this book he has so classified the elements revealed by that analysis as to give them a high scientific value, His book is almost as systematic as a treatise upon one of the exact sciences, and stands in fine contrast to the rambling, ethical discussion of which we hear so much and which leads us nowhere. How systematically Mr. Bierbower has gone to work appears from the very opening passage of the book.—*Chicago Daily News.*

Natural Religion and Other Sermons.—By JAMES VILA BLAKE. Cloth, 12mo, about 300 pages, $1.00. *Ready in October.*

A Grateful Spirit and Other Sermons.—By JAMES VILA BLAKE. Cloth, 12mo, pp 303, $1.00.

One of the remarkable things in these sermons is the union of freedom and boldness with reverence. . . . Another remarkable thing is the union of much careful reading—in prose and poetry apart from beaten tracks—with much homely observation of outward things and of men's lives.—*Christian Register.*

Happiness from Thoughts and Other Sermons.—By JAMES VILA BLAKE. Cloth, 12mo, 297 pages, $1.00.

Mr. Blake is predominantly a moralist of a true and pure strain, but a poet as well, and his moralizing on life is neither trite nor dry, it is such as to strengthen a deep and sober confidence in the Eternal Righteousness.—*Literary World.*

Helps for Home Nursing.—Second edition, revised. By IRENE H. OVINGTON. Cloth, square 18mo, 115 pages, 50 cents.

This little book deals in an eminently practical way with the simplest but often the least-known phases of home nursing.—*Christian Union.*

Charles H. Kerr & Co., Pubs., 175 Dearborn St., Chicago.

BOOKS OF RELIGION AND SCIENCE.

Our Heredity from God.—Lectures on Evolution. By E. P. Powell. Cloth, 12 mo, 416 pages, $1.75.

> It comes nearer being the hand-book of evolution, adapted to those who not only are looking for a clear summary of the evidences of evolution in the physical world, but are anxious to know its bearings upon morals and religion, than any book we know of.—*Unity, Chicago.*

> Altogether the book is the most cogent, candid, and absorbingly interesting of the many discussions of this momentous doctrine, by a thinker who both sees and states clearly its tremendous import. *Chicago Times.*

Liberty and Life.—Seventeen discourses on the applications of scientific truth to morals and religion. By E. P. Powell. 12mo, 208 pages, cloth, $1.00 ; paper, 50 cents.

> Strong, even, bold essays on ethical and religious subjects. They are the work of a man of vigorous intellect, who has studied the doctrine of evolution long and carefully, and has not found it necessary to abandon all his old reverences. The discourses are full of interest to the casual reader by reason of their fund of anecdote and biographical citation, and to the seeker for religious and moral truth they offer many helps.—*Literary World.*

> Seldom has a stronger indictment against dogmatic theology been so carefully drawn, or so successfully proved.—*Detroit Sunday News.*

The Evolution of Immortality.—Suggestions of an individual immortality based upon our organic and life history. By C. T. Stockwell. Third edition, with appendix. Cloth, 12mo, 104 pages, 60 cents.

> A thoughtful little book, which considers the growth of human being from embryological and cell-life up to the origin and evolution of consciousness, and, noting at every step the anticipation of the next, is justified in looking forward in the same line from the present point. It is worth reading.—*Atlantic Monthly.*

> The line of argument is comparatively new, and so well presented as to be profoundly interesting.—*Chicago Inter-Ocean.*

Charles H. Kerr & Co., Pubs., 175 Dearborn St., Chicago.

BOOKS OF POLITICAL SCIENCE.

The Rice Mills of Port Mystery.—By B. F. HEUSTON. A romance of the twentieth century, embodying the most telling argument against a protective tariff that has appeared in many a day. 12mo, 206 pages; cloth, $1.00; paper, 50 cents.

It is a strong showing for free trade, and any one desiring to get posted and crammed with good arguments should read it.—*Detroit News.*

The author has clearly made a hit. . . . It is a clever and ingenious production, and its issue opportune on the eve of another "campaign of education."—*Madison Democrat.*

Most entertainingly written, and will be as enjoyable to the general reader as it will to the economist.—*New Orleans Sunday States.*

Manual Training in Education.—By JAMES VILA BLAKE. A summary of the reasons why manual training should be made a part of the public school system. Square 18mo, 94 pages; cloth, 50 cents; paper, 25 cents.

Progrses From Poverty.—By GILES B. STEBBINS. A review and criticism of Henry George's "Progress and Poverty," and "Protection and Free Trade." Square 18mo, 64 pages; cloth, 50 cents; paper, 25 cents.

The Social Status of European and American Women.—By KATE BYAM MARTIN and ELLEN M. HENROTIN. Square 18mo, 47 pages; cloth, 50 cents; paper, 25 cents.

A capital little brochure for people who take a serious interest in the tendencies of American society.—*New York Independent.*

Why Government at All?—A philosophical examination of the principles of human government, involving a consideration of the principles and purposes of all human association. By WILLIAM H. VAN ORNUM. Cloth, 12mo, $1.50. *In preparation.*

Charles H. Kerr & Co., Pubs., 175 Dearborn St., Chicago.

BOOKS OF POLITICAL SCIENCE.

The Coming Climax in the Destinies of America.—By LESTER C. HUBBARD. 480 pages of new facts and generalizations in American politics. Radical yet constructive. An abundant supply of new ammunition for the great reform movement. The text-book for the Presidential campaign of 1892. Cloth, $1.50; paper, 50 cents.

It is an intensely interesting book, and as usual is only indicative of the colossal forces that lie behind it. . . . Aside from any discussion of specific measures the book is a striking one as an arraignment of present conditions.—*Chicago Times.*

The author is a prophet, or a "calamity screamer," according as the reader is of radical or conservative views, but his message is well and earnestly given, and as he has for years been a close student of the great labor movement, he is worthy of a respectful hearing.—*St. Louis Republic.*

As a vivid reflection of the universal unrest of the masses and portrayal of their wrongs it is unequaled by any book which has resulted from the rush of events which darken and thicken like clouds on the horizon on a summer day.—*Midland Journal.*

An Ounce of Prevention to save America from Having a Government of the Few, by the Few, and for the Few. Considerations in favor of a succession tax and a system of public manual training schools. By AUGUSTUS JACOBSON. Paper, 50 cents.

This is a small book, as books go nowadays, for it may easily be read through at a sitting. But it demands comment out of all proportion to its size, for it is both original and powerful. The author's style is clear, crisp, and concise. . . . The plan is a brilliant one. It has many excellent points. We admire its author's enthusiasm for the manual training school.—*Science*, New York.

Mr. Jacobson's book is scintillant with ideas on the labor question, in which he seems to be thoroughly versed.—*Evening Wisconsin*, Milwaukee.

A thoroughly sensible study of the labor question.—*Journal of Education*, Boston.

Charles H. Kerr & Co., Pubs., 175 Dearborn St., Chicago.

BOOKS OF RELIGION AND SCIENCE.

First Steps in Philosophy: Physical and
Ethical. By WILLIAM MACKINTIRE SALTER. Cloth, 16mo, $1.00.

This little book aims to answer in a thorough-going and scientific way two fundamental inquiries, What is Matter? and What is Duty? Clear notions on these points constitute, in the author's judgment, indispensable preliminary steps to any sound thinking in philosophy. He avoids technical language and puts his thoughts in simple and popular form. The book is not so much for philosophers as for ordinary men and women who are feeling their way to an intelligible and satisfactory view of the world.

Religion and Science as Allies, or Similarities of Scientific and Religious Knowledge. By JAMES THOMPSON BIXBY, Ph. D. Paper, 12mo, 226 pages, 30 cents. Cloth, 50 cents.

The best book published on the relations of Science and Religion.—*Christian Union.*

We have felt much gratification in the perusal of Mr. Bixby's argument. It is written in a highly commendable spirit and with a good general knowledge and appreciation of philosophic data, and its rich suggestiveness will be found to be by no means one of its least important merits.—*New York Times.*

The Unending Genesis; or Creation Ever
Present. By HENRY M. SIMMONS. Paper, square 18mo, 111 pages, 25 cents.

Here the story of the creation is told in a reverential, loving spirit, showing clearly how evolution has been going on for hundreds of centuries, and must still go on, and proving how one overruling power works through all, and with a perfect and mathematical precision.—*Unity.*

Evolution and Christianity. A Study. By
J. C. F. GRUMBINE. Cloth, square 18mo, 75 pages, 30 cents.

Mr Grumbine's statements are sound and well put. His book is the fruit of wide reading and investigation. It is a helpful one, is thoroughly interesting reading, and its presentation of the relation between evolution and Christianity includes much valuable thought.—*Buffalo Express.*

Charles H. Kerr & Co., Pubs. 175 Dearborn St., Chicago.

www.ingramcontent.com/pod-product-compliance
Lightning Source LLC
Chambersburg PA
CBHW021343230426
43666CB00006B/395